Never Give Up

Never Give Up

◆

A biography of Thomas L. Thomas

Cheryl Price

iUniverse, Inc.
New York Lincoln Shanghai

Never Give Up
A biography of Thomas L. Thomas

iUniverse, Inc.

For information address:
iUniverse, Inc.
2021 Pine Lake Road, Suite 100
Lincoln, NE 68512
www.iuniverse.com

ISBN: 0-595-33134-3 (pbk)
ISBN: 0-595-66752-X (cloth)

Printed in the United States of America

For my wife, Marie.

Thomas L. Thomas

Contents

Acknowledgments

I wish to acknowledge the assistance of Barry A. Smith for his artwork with the photographs that helped illustrate this biography of Thomas L. Thomas. He was able to computer enhance photos that were almost 100 years old in some instances and meld them into this life story. The remarkable memory of Thomas L. Thomas made this book not only a story of his life but made the times of the Depression and World War II come alive.

Robert E. Doherty not only read the completed manuscript and wrote the foreword, he also plied his craft as an experienced editor on my behalf. He is author of a history of the 96th Bomb Group, *Snetterton Falcons* and throughout the 1990's he reviewed books on the air-war for the "Stars & Stripes" newletter. In 1995 he won the TELLY Award in History for the video documentary, "Behind The Wire."

Thanks are due to my mother, Malvina Price who read and reread this manuscript and provided careful proofreading and encouragement during the process of preparing and writing.

Foreword

The recent wave of interest in World War II subjects created by the likes of Stephen Ambrose, Steven Speilberg, Tom Hanks and Tom Brokaw appears to have crested and is now ebbing. However, thanks to journalist Cheryl Price's persistent questioning of a kindly neighbor over the years *Never Give Up* merits inclusion in the better literature of WWII.

Whereas Ambrose wrote about the participants of D-Day, while Hanks and Spielberg concentrated on a special patrol and Brokaw presented a cross-section of service men and women, Cheryl Price telescopes downward through the military collectives to provide us with society's lowest common denominator one person.

From an orphanage during the Depression, through the college years and marriage—both interrupted by war through air combat and horrendous POW experiences, Tom Thomas returned to America as just one of twelve million veterans. There were opportunities, but there were obstacles too. The crucible of combat had raised the bar of achievement for him. He could take lemons and make lemonade. His ensuing successes equate him with the postwar generation depicted by Michael Bennett's *When Dreams Come True*. Indeed, Major Thomas's life brings to mind a famous quote from American ace, Joe Foss: "Those of us who lived have to represent those who didn't make it."

—Robert E. Doherty

Military Writer and Historian

Preface

I have known Thomas L. Thomas for many years. He has been a friend of our family. He would often talk of events that occurred when he was in the Army Air Corps and I tried for years to have him tell his story. For almost eight years, he refused to even consider the idea. He would often ask, "Who would be interested in me?" To which I would always reply, "There are many who want to know your story. You have a lesson to teach future generations."

I hope that his story will remind people that one of the greatest legacies of what Tom Brokaw called "The Greatest Generation" is their spirit and sacrifice for their ideals. They had and continue to have a vision of America that goes beyond the headlines in daily newspapers. These men and women who served during World War II had dreams to fulfill. Many lost their lives. However, others went on to pursue their dreams and have left a legacy for future generations.

I hope that this telling of one man's struggles will awaken others to the need to pursue their dreams and leave their own legacy for America.

—Cheryl Price

1

War and Survival

Thomas L. Thomas. Thomas L. Thomas. Each step in the snow reminded him of who he was. Even the cold, the bitter cold, seemed to echo his name, his past and the present. Who was he? A soldier, a prisoner of war in Nazi Germany, a man who had faced death before. Would he survive this winter that had burst forth in 1945 Germany?

He could scarcely see ahead of himself. The snow clung to his feet and his face felt numb. His eyes burned from the wind and cold. Ice coated his eyebrows and moustache. On either side of the snowy trail, he saw bodies of prisoners who had sunk into the deep snow. Yet, somehow he continued.

Again, his footsteps echoed his name—Thomas L. Thomas, Thomas L. Thomas. Marie, his wife, called him T. L. However, he was more than a soldier caught in the icy retreat of old German guards and Nazi fanatics. His life had been a matter of survival. Could he survive this death march? He imagined others must wonder the same thing about themselves.

Who are you? Who are you? The tramp of his feet and the crunch of snow seemed to envelop him. He thought of his brothers, his sisters. The faces of his brothers swirled around him in his memories. His father, his mother—they were long gone. He would not join them this day, he vowed. Instead, he would keep faith with his past and his future.

Thomas had promised himself a future long ago when his mother abandoned him and his brothers in an orphanage. He would not give up on those sacred dreams of childhood. Now that he was an adult, a soldier, he could not collapse in those inviting snow banks and give himself over to the freezing sleep of eternity.

Oh, but it looked inviting. It would be so easy to stop, to lie down and allow his aching body to rest.

No, don't be a fool! If you lie down, you'll never get up! He slapped his hands against himself and forced himself to continue. As the snow swirled around, he

1

thought about the past—the years in the orphanage, his struggles to attend college during the Depression and the violent interruption to those years when World War II became a part of his life.

It was not so long ago. Or, was it? No, he remembered it as if it was yesterday.

Thomas was born at Home on the South Side of Chicago to Tom Thomas and the former Lillian Beyers on October 18, 1917. His father's family came from Greece. His mother's family was German and Thomas sensed a split in the family at an early age, a split along ethnic lines.

In Greek, his father's last name was Papadotis. Before his father married, Lillian Beyers insisted that Thomas's father change his last name to Thomas. His father did, but that did not seem to be enough to please the German side of the family. His parents seemed to have overcome their different ethnic backgrounds to provide a stable environment for the family. Thomas remembered living above a bakery and a butcher shop until his father purchased a home on the city's South Side.

In his mind's eye, he could see his childhood in Chicago. The family had lived in the Greek community where his father owned and ran a Greek merchandise store and restaurant. Just before his father died, he bought a "Moon," one of the most luxurious cars available in the 1920's. It had a Rolls Royce style grille with a rampant lion raised as if to do battle. The interior was handmade in St. Louis. The roof of the car reminded young Thomas of an elongated, flat hat. However, unlike other manufacturers of the day, the Moon had not been built like a buggy with an engine attached. Instead, it boasted a six-cylinder engine and detachable wheels and Lockheed hydraulic brakes.

For all of its refinements, what Thomas remembered most was the soft leather upholstery. He used to run his hands across it, admiring its smooth texture and the ebony interior. His father had taken such pride in the purchase of the car. His mother had worried about its cost. However, for his father, it was a symbol of his success in Chicago.

The elder Thomas died July 10, 1924, when his son, Tom, was six years old. At that time, the family numbered six children. In chronological order, the family consisted of William, who was two years older than Thomas. After Thomas, came his sister, Mary, who was two years younger than he; then Richard, who was four years younger; another brother, Frederick and a second sister, Elizabeth (Betty). Betty was born just before his father died.

Later, when Thomas reached adulthood and looked back on his father's death, he thought his father had died from a holdover from the great flu epidemic that had swept the country in 1918-1919. His father caught a cold and from there it went into pneumonia. In the 1920's, few survived an attack of pneumonia. Antibiotics were unknown and the discovery of penicillin did not take place until 1929.

With the loss of his father, Thomas's family life changed dramatically. He, his three brothers, and his sister, Mary became residents of the German Evangelical Home for Children and Old People's Home in September 1924. Instead of having his own home and his own possessions, Thomas entered a life where all he had was shared with others.

It was only a month after his father's death that the Thomases were taken to the Home by his mother, grandmother and great-aunt. His great-aunt owned a car and she drove them to the small farming community of Bensenville. He remembered the drive. The car was strangely quiet. William, his elder brother, said little. His mother sat in the back seat looking straight ahead as if afraid to say anything to the other members of the family.

To Thomas, she seemed as if she was in another world. He would occasionally look at her drawn features and pale face, and then shift his gaze back to the terrain they were crossing. As the Thomas family left the crowded urban environment of the city, they came across small villages and towns that seemed to sprout out of the prairie lands to the west.

The original Bensenville Home was built in 1895. At the time it was a small structure, only 40 by 84 feet. In 1901, an addition was added to the east of the building. It was to this Home, with its new addition, that Thomas and his family came.

As they approached the building, his first impression was the building dwarfed the landscape around it. It stood four stories high. A bell tower and another tower reached high above a sloping roof. When they drove closer he could see two staircases leading up to the first floor. In the distance, beyond the building, he could see orchards. A dirt road led to the entrance. When they drew nearer, he saw the yellow brick of the building.

"Why are we here?" Thomas asked his mother.

There was no response. Instead, she continued to look straight ahead, and he watched with surprise as a grim, determined look spread over her features. Something wasn't right. He sensed it. But what was it?

Thomas looked toward the strange building. It seemed forbidding. His great-aunt parked the car and the family disembarked and walked toward the structure. Close to the front entrance were several trees. The trees' leaves covered the limbs like protective shells. Thomas barely noticed the residents of the home looking out the windows. Instead, he slowly followed his mother inside.

"I remember mother and grandmother saying good bye to each of us and the darkness closing in as evening approached," Thomas recalled as he continued tramping through the snow.

"Thomas, you will stay here," his mother said. "I cannot continue to support the family like your father did."

She did not hug him. She just bent down and took his hand for a moment, rose stiffly and joined his grandmother near the door. Thomas started to follow her. Someone, was it William? grabbed his hand and held him back. It was then that he realized that he, his brothers and one of his sisters were not to accompany her back to Chicago. He looked around frantically at the dark interior of the building. It appeared stark and cold.

Thomas knew his father had died but until now he thought he and the rest of the family were only out for a jaunt and would soon return to their home on the South Side. He looked toward his mother, unwilling to believe she could abandon his brothers, his sister and himself to strangers.

"You will be well taken care of," she said from the doorway before she and his grandmother exited the building. Thomas stood in the hallway staring at the door that had closed behind them. When his mother and grandmother left them, all the Thomas children had with them were the clothes on their backs. There was no suitcase to carry to another room. They had nothing with them to remind them of their father or the life they had once led.

Perhaps that was to make the separation easier, or maybe it was so he and his brothers and sister wouldn't suspect that they were being taken away from the home they had known when his father was alive. Thomas only knew that from that moment on he felt as if he no longer was a member of a normal family.

Someone took his hand and began guiding him up to the fourth floor. There was no time to think, no time to protest. Thomas realized that with every step he took he no longer was connected to the family he once knew.

That first night, Thomas entered a room that housed 20 boys. He had never shared a room with so many. When the older boys showed him around the Home the next day, he became aware of the playroom, the kitchen, the dining room and the quarters housing older residents and the girls.

His brothers and he were assigned to the section of the Home that housed boys. His sister, Mary, was taken to the girls' residence. The other boys tried to make him feel at home, but he felt abandoned. He would always remember that first night away from his childhood home in Chicago. When he looked around the dimly lit attic room that housed them, he felt as if he were truly alone. He tried not to cry. He knew it would do no good.

The way his mother had left him shocked Thomas almost to the point where he did not want to talk or communicate with anyone. In time, he came to look upon Bensenville as his family, but not during those first months at the Home.

2

Orphaned and Feeling Alone

The Bensenville Home stood on 130 acres of land. At the turn of the century, Bensenville was farm country. However, changes were beginning to sweep away the farm environment. The village of Bensenville was changing from a farm community to an area housing truck farms.

As Bensenville changed during the early nineteen hundreds, it found it was keeping pace with other rural communities in the country. A country that prided itself on farming was leaving its rural roots behind. Only 45 per cent of the land in the United States was rural when the 20th century began and at the turn of the century, Bensenville barely numbered 800 people. It still was considered a village. And, life within the village moved at a slower pace in comparison to the big city of Chicago to the east.

Grass, trees burdened with ripe fruit, a nearby baseball field, and the trees that flanked the Home created a far different world than the crowded city of Chicago with well over one million inhabitants.

Thomas did not know what to expect in these new surroundings. During the days that followed however, he became aware of the sights and smell of his new home. He and his brothers and sister came to Bensenville in September when the scent of the ripening grain wafted through the air.

He did not want to forget the teaming metropolis of Chicago. It was a reminder of his past. It meant he had a home, a room of his own, a father and mother. Yet, his mother had left him among strangers. It was as if she rejected him and his brothers. His sister would return to live with his mother but Thomas and his brothers were left to themselves in Bensenville.

He never forgot that first evening when he was led away to a room high in the attic of the Home. In that room he discovered a narrow bed, lights casting an eerie glow on the Spartan quarters and 20 other boys sharing his room. During those first days, he clung to his memories of Chicago; afraid that if he forgot Chicago he would lose his last recollections of his Father. Yet, already his father's features were becoming hazy reminders of his past. He mustn't let that happen.

Thomas soon fell into the routine at the Home. Each day the tower bell called the residents to meals and prayers. Breakfast began at 7:30 a.m. At 12:30 p.m. came lunch. At 5:30 p.m. they assembled for dinner. Bedtime came at nine o'clock. If he arrived late for a meal, he knew he would find the door closed and would do without the meal. The older residents sat on one side of the dining room, the children on the other. The staff and the superintendent, an ordained minister, sat at their own table. Food was plentiful and meals served family style with the children assigned to small tables.

During birthdays, the person whose birthday it was shared a cake with the other children at his or her table. Thomas had always shared what he had with others. However, he soon learned that if he received a gift of candy from infrequent visits of his mother he should grab a piece for himself first. Otherwise, the box would be returned to him empty.

The staff of the Home expected order and cleanliness. The tile of the hallway floor was waxed by hand. Down on his knees, Thomas helped scrub and wax those floors repeatedly until they shown like a mirror. In the room where Thomas lived, row upon row of beds looked up at overhead lighting. However, he spent little time in the cramped quarters. Activity in the Home was centered outside his bedroom.

He was assigned a set time to bathe in the showers in the basement. The regimen reminded him that there were no close ties like he knew when he lived with his parents. No one tucked him in at night. Each night, before he closed his eyes, he would see boys his own age sleeping in their own beds beside him.

He adjusted—adjusted to a life that at times seemed cold and uniform but at other times reflected the warmth of an extended family. For the next ten years he slept in a brown metal bed and stored his few possessions in a narrow storage locker. He and the other boys had only a few shirts and slacks. The only time he owned a suit was at the age of 13 for confirmation. He quickly outgrew it and didn't own another suit until he left the Home.

Despite being in a room with boys his own age, Thomas felt alone. Rather than betray his feelings, he withdrew into himself. His refusal to communicate almost resulted in his being placed a year behind the boys his own age at school. The public school wanted to put him in kindergarten. However, when they tested the six year-old, they found out he had been in first grade before coming to Bensenville.

The Home only allowed limited visits by relatives and because of this restriction, Thomas's mother came to visit the boys only once a month. He began to regard her as a distant figure. She was no longer a part of his life, not only did he lose his ties with his mother, but also his brothers and he soon began to lose the feeling of being a whole family. They lived at the Home together, but in different rooms and with different people who were literally closer to them than their own brothers.

Lillian Beyers Thomas was now a hostess and waitress at Fred Schmidt's restaurant on the South Side of Chicago. Betty, his youngest sister, stayed with Thomas's grandmother in the City. Mary, his other sister, remained at the Home until about 1932 when she went back to Chicago to join his mother, grandmother and her younger sister.

The boys' dormitory was up in the attic. The girls' dormitory was on the other side of the building. To the boys, it looked like a castle and that's what they called it The Castle. The elderly, in the Home, lived on the first two floors. The rooms for the adults were of different sizes. Some were for couples. Others held singles. Down in the basement, there was a dining room, a kitchen, a playroom and the showers.

The good thing about the home was when you were out there it seemed like some of the older people would adopt you, Thomas recalled. He remembered an elderly woman, a resident of the Home, who was particularly kind to him. There were many that seemed to take the younger residents under their wings.

We called her *Grossmutter* or Grandmother, he smiled at the memory. You'd always go to your grandmother, if you had to have socks darned or anything sewn. It seems like that happened to each of the boys and each of the girls. We had our own particular grandmother who would look after us. Because the home housed the elderly, death became a frequent visitor.

Whenever somebody died, they rang the old castle's bell. He could always tell how old the person was who died. If the person was 90 years old, they rang the bell 90 times. Those who rang the bell were the old folks who lived at the Home. It always left Thomas with a strange feeling when he heard the bell. Death seemed so final. Yet, he was always afraid that it would take one of the *grossmutters* who were so kind to them. If death took his *Grossmutter*—, what would he do? He didn't want to think of being without someone again. He didn't want to feel abandoned, as he had when his mother left him. This was a fear he tried to drive out of his mind. However, whenever he heard the bell ring it always returned.

As Thomas dealt with the changes that occurred at the Home, he found that he could adapt and thrive. Each day he looked out on a community that was self-sufficient. The Home had its own farm. It raised vegetables, beef cattle, milk cows, pigs and chickens. An experienced farmer ran the farm and some of the older residents helped. The belief in self-reliance was an unspoken part of life at the Home. Self-reliance was encouraged by the staff of the Home and by the elderly residents.

Thomas was assigned various tasks on the farm. One of his jobs was to help the chicken man clean out the chicken house and gather the eggs. The first thing he learned was to put glass eggs in the hens' nests so they would lay more eggs. Another job for the youngster was to work in the bakery, just below the chapel.

The bakery made its own bread and cakes. Thomas ran his tongue over his lips remembering how good the frosting was even now as he slogged through the deep snow as the Germans herded them toward the southern part of the country.

When he was older, Thomas helped in the fields hoeing corn. There were many times when he and the other boys disappeared among the ears of corn in August and didn't come out until they wanted. At other times, he'd ride the winch putting hay up in the barn and drop down on it.

"With all our chores, there's always something to lighten our tasks," he told his brothers one day. He learned early that he could make the world at Bensenville what he wanted. It could be dark and gloomy. Or, it could be bright with the possibilities a new tomorrow offered.

When Thomas first saw the gigantic cellar near the kitchen of the Home, he couldn't believe how many shelves held row upon row of jars and canned food. There were jars of preserved fruit and vegetables, baskets of onions and squash were on the floor. Piles of potatoes, carrots and cabbage encircled the cellar.

One old man, August, used to play his concertina every day. Thomas and the other children would gather around and listen to him sing. Hour upon hour he'd play German songs. He didn't talk much. When he did the children sat down on the bench and listened. They called him Gus. He was heavy, short and stocky. If it seemed as if he was going to stop playing, they'd call to him, "Hey Gus, play us another song."

August also made sauerkraut in a large vat from the cabbage grown on the farm. He'd ferment the cabbage with the brine from its own juice and salt. Then, he would get in there in his bare feet and walk around time after time. The only problem with Gus was he had no teeth. He used to chew tobacco and it would drip down into the cabbage.

"That's what makes the cabbage taste so good," Thomas joked to the other residents when some complained about Gus chewing tobacco and walking around the vat of sauerkraut.

The children also had their own vegetable gardens. They didn't have to tend the gardens, but the older people encouraged them to do it. After school in town, they had German school in the evening where they learned German.

Thomas soon learned that everybody who lived at the home was either full or part German. They went to church three times on Sunday—once to Sunday school, once to English Church and once to German Church. They also attended services every night in the Castle with the older residents.

His younger brother, Richard, liked to throw rocks at an old icehouse near the barn. There were glass windows at the top of the house and these were his favorite targets. Thomas would walk by his side and watch as Richard searched for just the right size rock that he could easily wield. The ice brought to the Home came from Lake Geneva, further to the west of Bensenville. When it arrived it would be placed on sawdust, layer upon layer, then used during the summer. There were other activities besides throwing rocks at the old icehouse. At one time, Thomas and some of his buddies were fooling around with a BB gun, shooting at various things.

"Let's see if we can shoot that chicken over there near the hen house," one of the boys said. Out of the corner of his eye, Thomas saw old man Thiele, the chicken man. Thiele bent over to do something to the chicken. At that moment, the boy with the BB gun fired.

"You hit him right in the butt," Thomas called out. In one motion, the boys turned and ran. The chicken man began yelling and chasing them. That's when profanity in German became a part of his vocabulary.

◆   ◆   ◆

It was strange how all theme memories of Bensenville and life at the Home came to mind so vividly on this cold winter's evening in Germany, Thomas thought. Maybe it was because he was in Germany and had been raised in a German "Home."

◆   ◆   ◆

Each day when they walked to the public school, about three-quarters-of-a-mile away, the boys' superintendent accompanied them. He was a retired Prussian military officer. He made them walk, not quite march, in pairs, all the way to school, while he rode along on his bike.

The school, a two-story building with an English style basement, was a combination grade school and high school. Four rooms on the second floor housed the high school, with one room for each grade. The grade school was on the first floor. There were four rooms on the main floor housing four grades and four rooms in the basement housing four more grades. By the time he got to the fifth grade, a two-room trailer was added outside the building. In it was a potbelly stove in the back corner of the room to keep the students warm.

One kid, Otto Schmidt, lived on a farm and brought his own lunch every day to school. Quite often, it was Limburger cheese and just about an hour before lunch he would take it out of his lunch bucket and put it right near the stove. Soon the warming cheese began to give off its own distinct aroma. It stunk up the whole room. Thomas swore the smell was so bad that anyone passing by the small schoolroom would get the terrible whiff of warm Limburger cheese.

During the fifth grade, Thomas found his grades improving. He gained more confidence in himself and began talking more. Sometimes his teachers did not appreciate his comments, especially when he yelled out, "Somebody let go a stinker."

The girl in front of him turned a beet red. And, the teacher sent him back to the Home with instructions to report to the superintendent.

"What are you doing here, Thomas?" the retired Prussian officer asked upon his arrival.

Thomas reluctantly explained what had happened, expecting any minute to receive a whipping for his actions.

Instead the officer roared with laughter and dismissed him. Thomas hurried out of his presence, afraid the man would change his mind. Just before he closed the door behind him, Thomas glanced back. The superintendent was still shaking his head and laughing.

When he entered the sixth grade, his nemesis, a teacher named Ellsworth, called him up to the front of the class. He had just smarted off with some wise remark that she didn't like. There she stood—ruler in hand.

"Thomas, you know the rules. Come here," she demanded.

He approached the front desk and waited.

"Stick out your hand," she ordered.

She raised the ruler and slapped his hand a couple of times. The ruler broke and he started laughing. That was the wrong thing to do. He could see the anger rising in her face. She walked over and picked up a tri-cornered ruler. Then, she really let him have it.

3

Growing in Confidence

Thomas was just entering the fifth grade when another event took place that left a lasting imprint on his life. A benefactor of the Home donated 15 to 20 different instruments to the children so that the younger residents would have an opportunity to form a band. Bensenville high school bandmaster, Lynn Huffman, gave lessons on how to play each instrument.

Thomas had often heard the music sung in chapel. However, he had never even held a musical instrument in his hand. He looked at the instruments with a mixture of curiosity and fear. Did the bandleader really expect him to play one of these instruments? Even if he could learn, he was sure that he wouldn't be able to play well enough to become a member of the band because he had buckteeth. His teeth projected outward, making it almost impossible to properly blow into an instrument.

One day when the bandmaster was talking to him about the various instruments he told Thomas that if he played the French horn it would push his teeth back.

"The French horn has a very small mouthpiece. In order to play it, you have to push hard against it," Huffman explained.

He was right. Over time Thomas noticed his teeth were gradually being pushed back. "It was almost as if the effort of pushing against the mouthpiece changed the way I looked at myself."

As he practiced, he began to notice a difference in his skill with the horn and in his appearance. It didn't push his teeth all the way back, but part of the way.

The band began to improve over time. As it spent more time practicing and playing together, the band began to get invitations to play at various church and harvest festivals. Thomas and his fellow band members found that by playing in the band they also had an opportunity to meet more townspeople their own age. The festivals were not only popular at the Home but with the town kids as well.

By joining town kids and Home kids together, they were able to make up a good-sized brass band.

During the summer and in the fall, the band played in Northern Illinois, Wisconsin and Indiana at church harvest festivals. Almost every church in their denomination had a festival in July or August. The band could play at a church on Sunday and return to the Home the same day.

Churches also came and sold things at the Home festival in Bensenville in the latter part of August. It was then that people brought in canned goods and donated them to the Home. Thomas soon learned that canned goods weren't the only items available at the festival. There were treats as well.

Thomas liked the homemade cakes and pies best. He and the other band members ate their fill of the desserts. The fresh taste of the layer cakes, the homemade ice cream, the coffee cakes and fruit pies made his mouth water at the very sight of them. After each church festival, canned peaches and canned tomatoes, potatoes, and a part of the farmers' crops were donated to the Home. It helped keep the place going.

There were also all kinds of food and handicrafts at the festivals. The older residents loved getting together with people their own age. When the festivities were over, all the monies earned were given to the Bensenville Home.

Those were some of the happiest days of his early years at Bensenville. Days seemed to flow into each other. Thomas grew tall and slim. He no longer minded being a part of such a large "family" as those residing in the Home. Now it seemed almost normal to have so many sharing a dormitory room. Yet, he knew it wasn't the norm of families. He could see that in the friends he made in Bensenville. They went home to parents and a different type of family, a family like the one he had known in Chicago.

Thomas barely felt the time pass. For recreation, he and the other children watched the cars that passed in the distance to see who could first identify a car before it came close.

They could tell what kind of a car it was just by the shape of it. He spotted Fords, Dodges or Chevies long before they came close to the Home. The grill-work on the cars was distinctive, almost as distinctive as the Moon that his father had owned so many years ago.

He'd watch the cars with anticipation. Was it a new car? What make was it? Would it stop at the Home? The road along side of the home was a two-lane dirt road. There weren't too many cars in the area, but Thomas remembered sitting around with the other Home kids and watching for cars hours on end.

He also took part in sports, like baseball or basketball. In the winter, he and the other boys ice skated. And in spring or summer, they would climb the trees in the orchards to get the fruit before it became an everyday part of their diet. When it came time for the fruit to be ripe, they took part in the harvest. He still remembered picking apples, plums and pears in the summer and fall.

During the summer, we played baseball. Every day after our chores were done, we played. We only had one ball. Our gloves were old. Nevertheless, we played until sundown. Sometimes we'd play in the morning and in the afternoon, he recalled. Even the town kids joined us. They knew we had this diamond built in the back and it was one of the few places in town where there was enough room to play.

If it rained, there were other activities. There was a library and Thomas discovered *Treasure Island*. He also read Jules Verne. After lunch, the staff of the Home set up a rest time and they read during this period and at night. With a library of books to choose from, Thomas could let his imagination soar. He prized the time he spent with a book propped up in his lap, engulfed in Sherlock Holmes or *A Connecticut Yankee in King Arthur's Court*. The works of Twain and Stevenson and the mysteries of Arthur Conan Doyle introduced him to worlds beyond the rural environment of Bensenville.

In September, the youthful residents went back to school. When I was in the Home there was no doubt about who we were, he recalled. In the public school, we were called the Home kids. However, he never felt discriminated against. He felt accepted.

From 1923 to 1929, Thomas still had a mother, no matter how distant she seemed. When he was 11, his mother died in a hit-and-run accident in Chicago. She was walking home along the side of the road when it happened. He and his brothers went to her funeral. On their return to Bensenville, Rev. Krause, who was in charge of the Home called the Thomas boys into his office and explained that they no longer had a mother.

One of the teachers said later, "You poor kids, you don't have a mother any more."

Thomas looked at her in astonishment. We were so used to being out at the Home from 1924 to 1929, when we rarely saw her, that it was not a great loss to us. She wasn't there anyhow.

Occasionally the Thomas brothers teamed up to defend themselves as a group. It didn't happen often, just enough to remind them that they had once been a part of another family.

On one occasion, four of us, my older brother, William; myself; my brother, Richard; and my brother, Frederick became involved in a fight with four other brothers—the Knoxes, Thomas recalled. It was one of the few times that he and his brothers joined together as the Thomas family, not the Bensenville Home family, but as Thomases.

Frederick was being picked on and he got into a fight. He called upon my brother, Richard, to help. When Richard helped, the next Knox brother got into it and Richard came to get me. Now, there were three Knoxes fighting three Thomases. It soon expanded to four Knoxes and four Thomases. By the time it was over, the Knoxes never bothered the Thomases again.

During his years at the home, Thomas awakened each morning at 6 a.m. He dressed and went down to the dining room to join his table for breakfast. He had been quiet the first few years at the Home. When he started seventh grade, he realized he was no different from anyone else. He realized he wasn't a dummy. In fact, he was one of the smartest kids in class. He found he had an aptitude for math. That aptitude attracted the attention of his teachers and they took an interest in his progress. For Thomas, this awareness opened new horizons. He felt a new confidence in himself and his abilities and he began to wonder what the future hold for him.

In 1927, the Home added a new building and in the process tore down the farm and the nearby icehouse. The boys and girls moved from the Castle to new quarters in 1928. The Castle remained, but it now housed only the elderly. The older building was viewed as a landmark by some. For others, it was a reminder of the orphans and the older peoples' place in the community.

The new Home consisted of three separate buildings—the girls' dormitory, the boy's dormitory and an administration building. The administration building, located in the center of the new Home, housed the offices, the kitchen, the dining room, a chapel and the gym. The boiler room was in the back. Underground tunnels connected the buildings.

In the new buildings, there were ten or 12 beds to a dormitory room, six beds on one side, six on the other. Each dormitory housed four different rooms. The quarters for the girls were almost identical to those of the boys. After the move took place, more maintenance of the new building meant more chores were required. The boys washed the dishes. The girls set the tables. Lawns needed mowing and the boys were also assigned chores in the laundry room.

During his first year in high school, Thomas began taking part in basketball. When he attempted to go out for football as a freshman, he broke his left ankle. The next year he went out for football again and broke his right ankle. The doctor told him he was too skinny for football because he never weighed over 140 pounds during his years in high school.

Since he couldn't play football, Thomas concentrated on basketball. In his sophomore year, he played on the high school senior basketball team setting a scoring record which stood for many years. Yet, his experiences in high school were set against the backdrop of the hard times that were beginning to affect the whole country after the stock market crash of 1929. He didn't need to be told that the Home was facing financial uncertainty. He could see it for himself. The Depression was leaving its mark on the orphanage—donations were down and he heard rumors that some of the orphans might be sent to live with relatives.

He hoped it wouldn't mean he'd have to leave Bensenville. He'd been there since he was six and barely remembered Chicago. While he had a distant aunt living in New York, his grandmother still lived in Chicago. He knew that if he was sent anywhere it would probably be to Chicago.

4

Return to Chicago

As the Depression hung on, Thomas and any other children who had relatives were sent to live with them. In 1933, a new phase of his life began when he moved into his grandmother's flat in Chicago.

Bensenville never had over 1000 residents. The residents were mostly farmers and retired farmers. There was a railroad yard where several Mexicans worked. However the diversity of employment and ethnic groups that marked the urban environment of Chicago was an area he was about to see and explore first hand. When Thomas finished his sophomore year in June, he left the school of 150 in Bensenville and enrolled in South Side Parker High School in Chicago, a school of 1500.

It was so different within the City. It seemed to him that he was like a new immigrant in a strange land. He just felt lost. The one thing that saved him was playing in the school's band. He also wanted to play basketball but couldn't because he couldn't afford the time.

At the time he moved to Chicago, his grandmother's partner, Frank Wells, helped run her apartment buildings. She owned two buildings, six flats altogether. His grandmother divided them up into smaller flats. So she ended up with ten, plus one whole flat for the family. Their flat consisted of three bedrooms. His sisters Mary and Betty lived in one room. Frank Wells had one room to himself and Thomas and his brother, Will, shared the other room. His grandmother changed the dining room into another room and stayed there.

While Thomas and his brother slept in double-deckers in one room, his two sisters had one big bed where they slept.

"It wasn't a bad deal, but when we got there my brother and I ended up being janitors," Thomas muttered. In the meantime Fred and Richard came to join the brothers in Chicago and to live in a basement flat in their grandmother's apartment building. But they didn't like it and soon moved back to Bensenville.

William took care of one building. Thomas took care of the other. Frank Wells helped the two brothers in the management of the flats.

When coal was delivered coal to the buildings, those delivering it would dump it in the back yard and Will and Thomas shoveled it in wheelbarrows and took it down to the basements of the buildings. Every day they cleaned the bathrooms, emptied the garbage from the back porch and when people moved out, William, Frank Wells and Thomas redecorated the apartments. By the time he was 16, Thomas knew how to wallpaper and make repairs.

"We were cheap child labor help. That was the way we earned our keep. We didn't get any money. We just had something to eat and a place to sleep," he said. At least his grandmother let Thomas and his brother go back to school.

Not long after Thomas's arrival, William returned to New York to live with his aunt. However, his brother did not stay with the aunt long and returned to Chicago.

While attending high school, Thomas and his fellow band members discovered the Chicago World's Fair. They would visit the Fair and also played with local marching bands in the city. Practically every organization in Chicago had marching bands or concert bands and he soon learned there was always a great need for French horn players.

"I have no trouble playing with a band and getting paid for it," Thomas told William. "I and the other band members usually earn a couple of dollars and carfare home".

At Parker High School, his ability in mathematics was recognized. In his senior year, he took an advanced mathematics class. The course emphasized advanced algebra and calculus and Thomas began to realize if he could easily handle the mathematics class, perhaps he could master other subjects as well.

In his senior year, he made the Owl Club, the National Honor Society of his day. It was one of his proudest achievements in high school. However, he felt no matter how much he accomplished academically it seemed to make no impression on his grandmother. She was more concerned about making a living than the achievements of her grandson in school.

When Thomas attended school, he took a sandwich to school with him for his lunch. He drank water because he couldn't afford to buy milk. His social life at the school was minimal. He didn't own a suit and had no money to spend on a date. Nor could he attend his high school prom.

Since there were four in the Thomas family with no parents, they qualified for relief. This eased the burden on the entire family. Although they received coupons for food, Thomas and the other members of his family never realized they were poor because everybody else was in the same boat during the Depression.

In 1935, he graduated from high school. He still lived with his grandmother and helped take care of the apartments. His aunts had a cottage on the Hudson River in New York, where his sisters spent the summer. Frank and his grandmother also went up there for several weeks during the summer. When they were gone, Will and Thomas ran the apartments. There was little time for entertainment. One day William and Thomas had a few extra dollars. His grandmother was gone so the brothers decided to buy a quart of ice cream. The last time Thomas had such a treat was in Bensenville. They sat on the front step of the six flat and devoured the contents between the two of them. It was such a rare experience that he felt as it it marked a high point of his life in Chicago.

While he heard of labor disputes during the Depression, Thomas saw little of the 60 sit-down strikes that occurred in Chicago. Instead, his world centered round the apartment complex until the end of 1935 when an opportunity came to secure a position with the Chicago Post Office. All he had to do was receive a high enough score on the Civil Service Exam. Thirty-five thousand people took the exam and 500 became postal employees. Thomas was one of them. In January 1936, he received his civil service appointment.

He began working for the post office in 1936 as a clerk-carrier, earning 65 cents an hour. This seemed a princely sum to the young employee. The minimum wage was $.25 an hour and he was well above that figure. And weekly wages for manufacturing or production worker positions were about $17 a week. So, he considered himself fortunate.

From the pay, he gave his grandmother money for food and bought his uniform. He quickly discovered that in his new position he could sub for other carriers when they were on vacation or sick and earn even more money.

He continued to live with his grandmother while he worked for the government. She never charged him rent but the understanding was he would continue to take of her apartments. It was an advantageous arrangement for both of them.

Thomas worked all of 1936.

"This can't be all there is for me," he told William. "I don't want to spend my entire life working for the government."

William sat on a hard-back chair listening to his younger brother. "Thomas, if you have a dream of doing something else, explore that dream and see where it leads," he advised.

Thomas began putting money aside. Without telling his grandmother, he started working extra hours in the evening. In the Polish neighborhood, there was a branch post office that needed clerical help in the evening. He would finish his routes about 3 o'clock, go over to the Polish area office and worked until 6 o'clock at night. In 1937, he had an opportunity to collect mail in the evening. He delivered mail as a regular mail carrier until 3 o'clock. Then he'd pick up mail from 3 to 11 in the evening. He worked 16 hours a day and arrived home at midnight exhausted.

He continued with this schedule and still took care of the apartments. Near the end of 1937, he decided he would follow his former teachers' advice and go to college. He continued to work two shifts through 1938 and at the same time sent an application into the University of Illinois and was accepted in the engineering program at the university.

"I'll use my math and become an engineer," he told a friend.

"You've got a steady job, Tom. Why go to college?" his friend asked.

"Because I don't want to be here the rest of my life. I want to do something more," Thomas replied.

"What more can you do but earn an honest buck?" his friend asked. "Don't be a dreamer. Stick with what you've got."

Leaving a paying job during the Depression wasn't an easy decision. There were over 13 million unemployed in the country in 1932. He had no idea what the totals might be in the late 1930s. He decided to ask his boss, the superintendent of the Stockyard Station at 41st and Halsted in Chicago for advice.

"If this is what you want, Thomas, go and get it," the superintendent said. "We'll try and work something out for you."

There was no doubt in his voice. It was as if he could see that there might be other opportunities available for the young employee.

Yet, Thomas still hesitated. He asked his brother, William, what he thought.

"Thomas, you have a desire to better yourself. If I had the same desire for an education that you have, I wouldn't let anyone stand in my way. No one."

Both his immediate boss and his brother were encouraging him to take the step that he wanted to take. He would never again question whether he was making the right choice. Of that, he was certain.

Thomas decided to go to downtown Chicago to talk to the postmaster, who happened to be a trustee for the Bensenville Home. Thomas waited all day to speak to him. When he had an opportunity to see him, he told him of his hopes and dreams. How he wanted to attend college and become an engineer.

"Thomas, you've been a top employee. I won't stand in your way. I think you should go to college. However, you must agree to come back to the post office during vacations in the summer and Christmas and during spring break."

It would mean he would have a position if he came back. The Post Office would actually hold a position for him. Thomas breathed a sigh of relief. "Thank you, sir. I appreciate what you're doing and I'll be here during those time periods."

This should answer any objections of my grandmother, he thought. I am not totally closing the door on a paying job. Instead, I am opening the door to being an engineer with the postmaster's blessing.

When he told his grandmother of his decision, he received no encouragement. All she could see was the hard times that existed and the many who were out of work. She could not understand him quitting a paying job to go to school, especially during the Depression.

"No member of our family has ever attended college," she said. "It is not for us, especially not now. Do you know how fortunate you are to even have a job?"

"I know. That is what makes this decision difficult, but can't you see what this means? I'll be able to have a career. I'll be able to use my skill with math as it was meant to be used," Thomas said.

She refused to listen, to acknowledge he had the right to pursue his dream. He looked toward Uncle Frank, hoping he'd help persuade her to the rightness of his decision, but Frank Wells face reflected the same emotion so apparent on his grandmother's face. To go to college was a rich man's luxury. It was not meant to be a part of the life of the Thomases. He sensed his grandmother and uncle's disgust at the idea.

"If you're so smart then go out on your own," his grandmother said. "But don't bother to come back here."

Thomas couldn't hide his shock at her response. To tell him he was no longer welcome in her home if he went to college was more of a rejection than he expected.

When he was six, he'd lost the support that a family provides when he and his brothers were placed in the Bensenville Home. When the Depression arrived he'd lost the protection of Bensenville. Now for the third time, he was losing the security of a home environment. This time he was on his own completely.

Lillian Beyers Thomas, baby Richard, Thomas L. Thomas, William Thomas, Mary Thomas and Thomas' father prior to 1923.

Thomas's father at the Beyers restaurant in Chicago about 1910.

William on the tricycle, Lillian and young Thomas in 1919.

Bensenville Home in 1924.

Bensenville Home with its new addition in 1929.

Thomas at confirmation (second row, second from left). He still lived at
the Bensenville Home at the time.

5

On His Own

Thomas went back to the room he shared with his brother. He looked at his face in the mirror. The face that looked back at him showed the strain of working two shifts a day at the post office. He could also see a determined set of his jaw in the rectangular feature. His brown hair was wavy. The eyes looked straight ahead as if challenging the future. He was still thin and wiry. However, he had filled out after his senior year in high school. No longer was he a thin, six footer, who weighed 140 pounds and set a high school basketball record in Bensenville. He now weighed 175 pounds. The work at the post office, lifting 60-pound bags of mail, had added muscle to his frame.

He hesitated. He so much wanted to have his family approve of his decision. Yet, he had to face the facts. His real family was gone, except for his brothers and sisters. Perhaps his father would have approved of his pursuing an education if he were still alive. Would his mother? Probably. His brothers? He already knew that they would support his decision. Despite the separations into different rooms and classes at Bensenville, they had not severed the tie of family completely.

Thomas turned away and removed a beat-up satchel from underneath his bed. Slowly, he began packing. There were not many clothes to pack—a few slacks, underclothes, and socks. He had one sport coat and a heavier coat for winter.

His mind drifted back to his grandmother. Why did she act the way she did? he wondered. She provided a roof over his head and food. Those were his wages for keeping up the apartments. He had not been completely without funds during his high school years. He earned some money by playing the French horn for various bands in the city. It meant husbanding the extra money he earned. No dating. He could not afford it. No going to the prom. Out of the question. Just go from high school on to work at the flats. And from high school, he had gone to work for the Post Office.

When the opportunity came along to earn a dollar a day in the 124th Field Artillery band, a part of the National Guard, he jumped at the chance. It meant four or five extra dollars a month.

He counted the money he had saved by working the extra shifts in the post office and playing in the band. A little over $500! If he could get a job on campus, it could see him through two years of college, perhaps more

Thomas completed packing his few belongings and walked out the door without another thought of the security he was leaving behind him.

◆   ◆   ◆

When he arrived at the University of Illinois, Thomas was amazed at how spread out the campus was. The engineering hall was right in front of a drainage ditch called Boneyard Creek. He soon found an area of independent housing a brisk walk from where the majority of his classes would take place. There he located a room at a cost of $15 a month. Another $15 went to purchase a year's athletic ticket. It would allow him to see football, basketball, hockey and baseball events during the year.

Thomas's room at the house was efficient. It contained two chests of drawers, a closet, two beds and a sink. Thomas hung up his sports coat and a pair of slacks. He then placed his winter coat in the closet and put his meager belongings in the chest. Two thirds of the chest remained empty. He decided he might as well use some of the drawer space for books and paper.

He shared the room in independent housing with another student, Shelby North. North was tall, dark-haired and well dressed. and dated the law dean's daughter. Whenever Thomas came back from class, he could tell when his roommate was there. North smoked a pipe and the smoke had a distinct maple rum scent that permeated the room.

Other men living in the house included Eugene Nave from Metropolis, Illinois and a senior majoring in math. Eugene was tall and skinny, with light blond hair. Thomas soon found out that he was a good talker, but hated studying.

As if by mutual agreement, Shelby and Thomas went their different ways. Thomas could not hope to compete with him in terms of a social life. He didn't have the funds for that. However, he was confident he could hold his own academically. He plunged into his classes, anxious to absorb as much as possible and make up for lost time.

I should have been here right after high school, he thought. Instead, I picked up and delivered mail. He felt the difference between him and the other college students was not so much in qualifications but in where he was from.

I'm a country bumpkin, a kid from a small town, Thomas reflected. But that won't stop me from succeeding. All I need is a chance. However, he knew that chance or luck rarely paid him a visit. "There's no such thing as luck, only hard work," he told himself.

The other fellows who resided in the house where he lived could not afford to be in a fraternity or live in a dormitory on campus. There were about a dozen in the house who formed a compatible group. Until Thomas could find a way to earn extra money at the university, he'd have to stretch his money.

The woman who ran the house was a good cook, but he couldn't afford to eat there.

Instead, he bought a weekly meal ticket for $5.50, which allowed him to eat at a downtown restaurant twice a day. On occasion, he would find his way to Kammeres, a student hangout on campus. It served coke and hamburgers and was directly across from the engineering building. Whenever he entered the combination bar and restaurant, he smelled the aroma of hamburgers, cigarettes and pipe tobacco. Beer labels covered the wooden walls of the building.

He paid the tuition of $35 a semester, bought his books and began looking for a job. It wasn't until his second semester that he found one as a waiter in a sorority house, Zeta Tau Alpha. If he had been less than six feet tall or stocky, he wouldn't have been able to secure employment there. The housemother insisted that all waiters be slender and six feet in height or taller.

The sorority provided his meals for serving breakfast, lunch and dinner. The House lay at the south end of the campus. The engineering school was at the north end. It was a long walk, but Thomas didn't mind. He had a place to live and meals to keep him going. It seemed as if things were finally going his way.

On the nights when the sorority had its parties, one of his jobs was to add booze to the punch. He stood with his back to the bowl and carefully emptied the contents of liquor bottles into it.

The housemother had to know this was happening, but she never said anything. When he wasn't attending classes, studying, serving meals at the sorority house or attending athletic events, he played pinochle with the guys at the house.

Then, something happened during his first year he hadn't counted on. He met a girl. Her name was Marie Grych. At five foot four, with short red hair, she reminded Thomas of the picture-perfect girl next door. She wanted to be a teacher and was taking courses at the university in education. It was her last year on campus. She'd already completed three years at Chicago Normal and attending the university would enable her to finish requirements for a degree. Unfortunately, she was dating Thomas's roommate and try as he might, she wouldn't have anything to do with him.

When Marie left the university, he obtained her Chicago address and telephone number. He would not call her until he was better situated. That meant waiting until he completed his first year.

His return to Chicago that first winter meant finding a room to share with a friend. He was unwelcome at his grandmother's place. His pride would not allow him to press the question of staying at her flat. Instead, he had the added expense of paying for a room with the funds he earned at the post office.

His plans had called for his earnings from the post office to supplement the monies he had saved while working before entering college. He was not able to put away the monies he earned during school breaks. Instead the earnings only helped pay for a room while he was in Chicago.

One of the members of the 124th Field Artillery Band, Harry Spears and his wife, Frances opened their home to him during the Christmas holidays. They allowed him to stay with them at a reduced rate.

Thomas was already thinking of the upcoming summer. When summer came, he hoped he would have an opportunity to replenish his depleted savings so he could continue at the university. Only then would he truly be able to provide for the cost of attending the University. His agreement with the Postmaster was a blessing, but it also was a problem.

Soon semester break would come. If he had to pay for room and board at that time, he would have even less money for school. Then, Gene Nave, who roomed at independent housing with him, invited him down to his home, just north of Metropolis.

The town where Gene lived consisted of four houses and a general store. Gene's home had no indoor plumbing or electricity, but Thomas barely noticed. His roommate's parents treated him like one of their own sons. Never had he felt so welcome. It was like having a family of his own. He was only there a week, then it was back to being on his own at the university.

The university was far more expensive than he had envisioned. He needed money to continue his education and must look ahead to his sophomore year. It was 1939. Where else could he earn money? His enlistment in the National Guard was up in the spring. He would have to re-enlist. He needed every dollar he could get and the Guard provided a means of earning money. Playing the French horn was a hobby, but a hobby that helped financially. So there were two extra sources of income. However the monies they provided were minimal compared to his expenses.

Do I need to worry about being called to active duty? he wondered. It was a chance he'd have to take. If he was called up, it would disrupt his education. That seemed unlikely.

I need the money, Thomas decided. There was no choice. He had to remain in the Guard.

The spring of 1939 proved to be the lull before the storm. In September, Hitler ordered the invasion of Poland. The Armistice of 1918 had proven to be only a pause before more fighting began on the European continent. Thomas gave little thought to the political and military movements overseas. His primary focus was on gaining his education in engineering. The war on the European continent was a world away. Like the other students, he hoped the United States could remain neutral.

If the country entered the conflict, it would certainly be more useful to have the educational background of an engineer. Aware of events, but somehow distantly removed from the growing turmoil, Thomas continued his studies. After his first year, his grandmother reconsidered allowing him to stay in her home. He made the dean's list and she offered to allow him to come back to the apartments but he refused. She hadn't written him at all during his year at the university. Now she was opening her doors to his return? He had too much pride to go back to her at this point.

"The only reason she made the offer was she saw my grades from my first year," Thomas told Eugene Nave. "I'll be darned if I will go back to her now."

Following the invasion of Poland by Germany in the fall of 1939, the government began plans for the institution of a draft for military service, which became law in 1940. The draft used a lottery system to see who would be the first selected for military duty. When the numbers were chosen on September 16, 1940, Thomas's number was one of the lowest at 115. The first 114 numbers were excused for various reasons including being married, employed in essential jobs or being unfit for duty. Although, he had a low lottery number, he wasn't called up immediately because of being in the Guard.

So far, so good, Thomas thought. He tried to keep the thought of being drafted at bay when he worked at the post office during the summer. He returned to school in the fall. For the moment, he could continue his studies. Other than the events of the war, his mind kept returning to Marie Grych. He couldn't get the thought of Marie out of his mind. In the beginning of his sophomore year

Thomas telephoned Marie and persuaded her to come back to the university for a dance.

"We seem to hit it off and I am going to see her every chance I get when I return to Chicago," Thomas told Eugene Nave. "I want to be more than a casual date for her. She's special."

He finished the first semester of his sophomore year and dropped out of school to earn money for the following fall semester. Would it effect his status with the draft board? He didn't know. He couldn't dwell on something he had no control over. He began to see Marie when he wasn't working at the post office in Chicago and was becoming increasingly interested in her.

He knew that he could never save enough money for college if he continued to have to meet the expenses of living in the city. Swallowing his pride, Thomas decided to live with his grandmother until the following fall when he would return to school. In the fall of 1940, he returned and finished his second year at the university.

Events in Europe were now moving rapidly. The newspapers reported the fall of Belgium, France, Luxembourg, the Netherlands, Denmark, Norway and Romania to the Nazis. Roosevelt was attempting to make the United States the arsenal for democracy. Yet, the president's budget during his third term also emphasized an awareness of the danger of the war spreading. The new budget provided more money for defense.

Thomas received word in the late fall of 1940 to report for duty on March 5, 1941, at the Armory in Washington Park, Chicago. His orders informed him that he would be shipped to an artillery battalion in the south. After reporting, he was sent to Camp Forest in Tennessee for a year of training.

"Here I am playing band music for a regiment," Thomas wrote Marie. The musicians were also supposed to be in the process of becoming combat ready. Band members were assigned to work with medics as stretcher-bearers. They also had to learn first aid.

Another aspect of military life became a reality to Thomas. The Army moved at the pace of a turtle, not a hare. And, at times he could scarcely see any movement. No one was in any hurry to become combat ready despite the fighting that raged overseas. The thought of all the men was we'd be here only a year. Then, we can return to private life. Thomas had the same horizon in sight. Serve for the year, and then return to college.

"I'll wait this out," he vowed. "The United States is not directly involved in this conflict. When my year is done, I'll get out and reenter college."

In the meantime, whenever he was given leave, he returned to Chicago to see Marie. When the Japanese bombed Pearl Harbor, Thomas and the others in the artillery unit realized immediately they were now in the war for the duration.

I could have stayed in the National Guard band with a field artillery unit, Thomas recalled as he continued the cold walk to the south of Germany. The unit was in the process of changing over from horse-drawn field artillery units to motorized units. The band was a nice, safe job. If he continued, if he didn't attempt to get involved with elements that might be called into combat, he could stay out of harm's way.

I can stay here until the end of the war, he thought. But what does that say of me? How will I look at myself later? He believed he had an obligation to his country. That obligation did not include playing it safe behind a French horn.

"I think I can do more good for my country elsewhere," Thomas told Marie when he visited her in December after the Pearl Harbor attack.

He took her to a jewelry store in Chicago. Though the country was engaged in war, the holiday season still hung over the city and the store was aglitter with expensive pearl necklaces and rings of every description.

"I have a friend who is going to marry soon. He's going to get engaged and he asked me what kind of a ring he should get his girl friend," Thomas said. "Give me some ideas for him. Help me pick out a ring for him."

Marie looked at him for several minutes. Then she picked out a simple diamond ring with a gold band. "If it were for me, I would choose that ring," she said.

Thomas gazed at the ring. It was a small stone, but it looked beautiful. He asked the price and then left.

I make only $36 a month as a sergeant, Thomas thought. How can I afford a ring like that? But, Marie loves that ring. And, that is the ring she will have.

Too soon, his leave was up and he returned to duty, but not before he had put money down on the ring. After his return, he applied for the aviation cadet program. He also applied to go to Field Artillery Officers Candidate School (O.C.S.). He did not hear from the cadets, but he was one of two men selected from the entire artillery regiment to go to O.C.S., at Fort Sill, Oklahoma.

As Thomas began his training at Fort Sill, he wished he had heard from the cadets. That was where he most wanted to serve. When he did hear from the cadets, he was already halfway through O.C.S. But he immediately went to his commanding officer and showed him the papers.

"We don't care what they say," the commander said. "You're in O.C.S."

"But I want to join the Army Air Corps."

The commander shook his head. "That's impossible. The only way you can do it is if you resign from O.C.S. Even then, there is no guarantee. We will send you back to your artillery unit and you may never have the opportunity of becoming a cadet. You would be better off staying here. There's no reason to take that chance."

"But what if it's something I always wanted to do, sir?"

The question remained unanswered. Thomas returned to his quarters to ponder his dilemma. And, like the time when he chose to leave his grandmother's home and went to the university, Thomas again felt he had no choice. He would have to resign.

6

Flying Solo

Thomas returned to the barracks. He sat and watched as the other men went in and out for classes. He envied them. They had a set objective, a goal within reach—complete OCS and receive an assignment as an officer overseas. And he, like he had so many times before, followed his dreams.

When would he quit looking for a rainbow and face reality? The commander said that there was no guarantee he'd even be able to enter cadet training. Why couldn't he accept that? Go along. Wasn't it easier? However, he knew in his heart that it was better to make the effort to succeed rather than wonder about not trying to become a cadet later.

He knew Marie would not want him to give up a sure thing. But, flying? It was another horizon to conquer, another dream to meet and fulfill. When he was at the Home in Bensenville, he had read of so many who made their dreams a reality. Each book he picked up as a child at the Bensenville Home spoke to him about the need to work hard and take chances. He had taken a chance by giving up the position at the post office. Now he wanted to fly. There was another world out there, a world that included the opportunity to fly.

The men in the barracks did not ask him why he wasn't attending class. They never asked what was happening to those who at one moment were a part of the training to be an officer and the next moment were no longer a part of the group. It was a subject that was never broached. It was akin to approaching a pitcher who was throwing a no hitter in the bottom of the eighth inning. They did not want to jinx the pitcher or themselves. Therefore, the subject remained off limits, even if he had wanted to tell them why he was leaving, he knew he couldn't.

In less than a week he left Fort Sill. The Army reduced him to the rank of sergeant and assigned him to a field artillery regiment in Brownwood, Texas. The unit was the 174th field artillery. It was part of the Dixie Division from the South.

I'm back where I started, Thomas thought, a French horn player in a military band. He hadn't wanted that after Pearl Harbor. He didn't want it now. It seemed as if the military was determined to place him in a box of their choosing, not his. He immediately applied for cadet training again. As he did so, he discovered that other members of his new battalion also dreamed of flying.

"The Army doesn't want us to join the Air Corps," one man told him. "Even if we have the necessary papers, they seem intent on preventing us from becoming aviation cadets. I'm not going to let them stop me though."

He agreed. If the men gave up, the Army would win. Thomas sensed that the Army was using delaying tactics to thwart them. It became apparent to him and the others if the would-be cadets could be delayed long enough; they could be assigned overseas. Then, there would be no recourse. Not one of them would be able to return and become a pilot. He and three others from the battalion learned that the Air Corps had set up a recruiting office in Dallas that was open on weekends.

"We can hitchhike to Dallas on Saturday," Thomas said. "Talk to the recruiters about our situation. Maybe then, we'll be able to join the Air Corps."

The others quickly agreed. They had no trouble getting a lift to Dallas. They located the recruiting office with no difficulty. He and the others walked in the door and showed the officer in charge their applications and acceptance for cadet training.

"We're on the books as accepted, but we can't get released from our present units," Tom told the recruiter. The man didn't seem surprised. Instead, he ordered them to take the required mental and physical exams.

"Return to your base and wait. You'll receive your orders," the recruiter promised.

Two days later Thomas received orders to report to Waco, Texas, to await assignment to aviation training in San Antonio. Instead of just four men leaving the artillery base, a dozen left Brownwood the same day to become flying cadets. As he left, he realized that none of the men ordered to Waco was less in rank than a sergeant. Others from Army bases near Brownwood joined them bringing the total of would-be cadets up to 25.

Upon entering the air base at Waco, he and the other cadets discovered the base wasn't even finished. The buildings still had glass windows with union labels on them. In order to see out of their new barracks, Thomas and the other men began scraping the labels off with a razor blade.

The commander of the base decided to put the 25 new arrivals to work. And not just any work, he delegated the worst jobs on the base to the newly arrived cadets.

"All of you are going on permanent KP," he told them.

"That is not in our orders, sir," said a technical sergeant. "You can only provide us with room and board—no assignments. We stay here until they assign us to San Antonio."

"You are not here for a vacation," the commander fumed.

"The orders say room and board. That's it, sir."

"I don't believe it." Thomas and the others waited as he read the orders. The commander's face became red with anger. He read and re-read the orders. Finally, he walked away.

"They cannot make us work," said a top sergeant. "But we can volunteer. Better to do something than just sit."

Thomas agreed. He found it difficult enough to sit and do nothing in civilian life let alone in the military. Most of the 25 new arrivals pitched in to help at the base, but they made it clear, they were volunteering. They weren't accepting the commanding officer's idea of permanent KP.

The only thing the base commander could require of the new arrivals was that they answered roll call on Monday mornings. Although the men "volunteered" to help on the base, many went home for a week then came back and reported at morning roll call. Thomas had no place to go so he remained at the base.

Every Sunday, he and some of the newly arrived recruits went to church in Waco. The First Baptist Church was the largest church in town. After services, Thomas and his friends waited outside to see if anyone would invite them to dinner. They were never disappointed. Not one had to return to the barracks and they looked forward to having a home cooked meal one day a week.

One of the most powerful families in the Waco area was the Howell family. Hilton Howell and his wife, Louise, invited Thomas to dinner the first Sunday he attended the Baptist church. When he saw their English style home, he was amazed at its size. Upon entering the front door, he saw fireplaces, chandeliers and wooden floors. The dining room and living room were immense.

Hilton Howell was an influential attorney and judge. He and his wife owned local radio stations in Waco and the surrounding area. They had three children, all boys. The youngest was four or five. The middle child appeared to be about eight and Junior, he was 12.

After the first invitation, Thomas became a regular dinner guest. He'd go to church with the Howells and they even picked him up on Saturdays when they went to their country club. While the Howells visited the club, Thomas watched the children. He enjoyed the company of the adults and liked their children as well. They even let him use their car to take the children swimming.

The Howells had a way of including him in their conversation and he found himself telling them of his family and growing up at the Home in Bensenville. He made sure they realized that he had been happy there.

"Thomas, I admire you," Hilton Howell said one day. "No place or circumstance has interfered with you pursuing your dreams. I hope you do return to school and become an engineer."

It's as if I've gained the support and acceptance of a family of my own, Thomas thought. In making the comparison, Thomas realized how much he longed for a family that had roots and its own home. He had been without those bonds too long.

Meanwhile at the base in Waco, a second lieutenant decided that if the Army couldn't assign the men duties at the base at least they could train them to be good soldiers.

"I'm going to see that you men know how to march and drill,' the lieutenant said as he assembled a group of 50 cadets. He put them through a simple maneuver where they marched back and forth, stood at attention, then did an about face.

Thomas was amused at the lieutenant's efforts. Finally a sergeant said, "Lieutenant, do you mind if we take over and do this ourselves?"

The lieutenant moved to the side and watched as the 50 men marched forward and back. They put on a close-order drill that was a picture of precision and order. When they finished, they stood at attention briefly, staring straight ahead. Then, placed themselves at ease.

"I can't teach you anything. I don't know half of what you're doing," the lieutenant admitted before turning on his heel and leaving.

◆   ◆   ◆

In August 1942, the would-be cadets began receiving orders to report to San Antonio. Thomas's orders came through in September. He just had time to say goodbye to the Howells before reporting to the San Antonio Aviation Cadet School. That was its proper name, but he and the men called it SADSAC.

Upon their arrival, the men took tests to determine whether they would be a pilot, navigator or bombardier. The highest score on the tests was a ten. Thomas scored a nine on pilot and navigator and an eight as a bombardier. He requested instruction to become a navigator. Instead, he was assigned to pilot training.

At San Antonio, upperclassmen and lower classmen lived in the same barracks. The upper classmen lived on the upper floor and the lower classmen beneath them.

Thomas wasn't allowed to walk across the base without being accompanied by at least one other cadet. He supposed it must be an effort to instill teamwork. If there were two men walking together, they were considered a pilot and copilot. If three, a pilot, copilot and navigator. If four, they included a pilot, copilot, navigator and bombardier. The least amount of men that could walk the base together were two, the pilot and copilot.

In the mess hall, he discovered he was not permitted to talk unless an upperclassman asked him a question. Otherwise, he had to sit up straight and eat as if he was making a square with his hand, moving it from the plate upwards until it was opposite his mouth, then bringing it to his mouth.

The new routines and procedures the men followed lasted from September through November. The San Antonio Aviation Cadet School was known as the West Point of the Air Force. Following the procedures for even three months was trying, and Thomas wondered how those appointed to West Point withstood four years of military training.

When he first applied to the Air Corps, the only people eligible for flight training were those who had two years of college. Thomas barely met the qualification for training at the time he was accepted in the Corps. As the war dragged on, the standards were lowered so high school graduates could enter training if they passed the exams. Thomas began to see the effects of this change in the latter part of 1942.

There were three steps to becoming a pilot—primary training, basic and advanced. Thomas was assigned to Sweetwater, Texas for primary flying school. Sweetwater lay 25 miles west of Abilene. The town was small, with a civilian airfield. The civilian trainers were responsible for the initial instruction of the new cadets.

As he grew accustomed to the feel of rolling down the runway, gradually pulling back on the throttle for lift off and flying across the Texas plains, Thomas became aware of the sweep of the land beneath him. High in the sky, he could barely make out the sagebrush and cactus below. Time and again, he took the plane up under the careful guidance of the civilian pilot, who eventually asked him to set the plane down completely on his own.

"Thomas I'm going for a walk. Take the plane up for 15 minutes and then land it," the trainer said one day.

Solo! He was actually going to solo! Thomas couldn't believe the moment had finally arrived.

He pointed the plane toward the runway and taxied forward, gaining speed. He felt the wind lifting the single wing of the plane into the afternoon sky. It felt so easy, so natural, just as he imagined it would feel.

Several hundred feet in the air, he circled the runway gazing at the single strip of the airport below him. How small it seemed. It made him realize how small man was in relationship to the world around him. There was barely a cloud visible on the horizon and Thomas felt as if he could touch the world outside the cockpit. He flew back and forth, losing track of time as he took in a world that had once been the primary realm of robins and eagles. Alone in the plane, he wondered what role he was destined to play in the war. Would he be bombing an enemy? Would he be a fighter pilot? It seemed so distant from the peaceful area around him.

Could 15 minutes have passed? he wondered. He looked at his watch. Close to 30 minutes had slipped by and he had to go back to the place from where he came. Reluctantly, Thomas maneuvered the plane into position around and began the descent.

Decrease your air speed. Steady. Don't let the wind catch it, he told himself. The ground came closer and closer. Bring the nose up, he told himself. Not so much. He worked the controls slightly adjusting his height and lowered the flaps. Almost there. He felt the wheels touch, reduced the speed until the plane rolled to a stop and turned off the engine. That was it. His first solo. Thomas sat there for several minutes savoring the experience.

He finally climbed out of the plane as his fellow pilots gathered around him. He'd almost forgotten what the first reward was for reaching this milestone—a dunk in a nearby pond.

7

Pilot to Navigator

After his first flight in November, Thomas spent all the time he could in the air. Between Thanksgiving and Christmas, he caught a cold and his airborne activities were curtailed. Behind in the number of hours needed to advance to basic training, he and some other aviators, including his buddy, Bob Thomas, were confined to the base during Christmas. When Christmas Day 1942 arrived, he and Bob tried to make up the hours necessary to qualify for basic training.

Flying on Christmas was not Thomas's idea of a Christmas present. However, he had no choice. He had to get his hours. In the morning, he took off and spent time circling the area around Sweetwater. Whenever he was in the air, he felt like he was in another world. He always marveled at the view from the cockpit. Looking away to the horizon, it seemed as if the flat plains of Texas stretched on forever.

He spent hours flying back and forth practicing various maneuvers, watching the still plains beneath the plane or soaring upward, then banking, and leisurely turning back toward the base. A few hours after noon, he put the plane down at the base and was just in time to meet Bob. They set off for Christmas dinner at the mess hall. As they fell in step, the base appeared deserted. There usually was someone walking around and it gave him an uneasy feeling. Thomas looked in every direction but he had the distinct feeling that the base had closed down. Even the control tower looked as if it was empty.

"There's a faint light from the control tower," Thomas said. "But I bet even that is at short staff."

When they approached the dining area, he could detect no aroma of food coming from the wooden building.

"It's closed," said Bob as he tried the door. He looked around to see if there was anyone they could catch a ride with to the nearest town. All they could see were cars pulling away from the gate.

"I never thought I'd see this base deserted," Thomas said. "Everyone must have taken off for the Christmas holiday."

"I think you're right, Thomas. It sure seems strange."

"Let's walk into town," Thomas suggested.

When the two cadets reached the center of town, they saw it was as empty as the base. "Well if nothing else, maybe we can hitch-hike to a town that has an open restaurant,"

Bob said. He stood on one side of the road, Thomas on the other. They waited. Neither cared what direction they went. The objective was to get something to eat.

An old Chevrolet drew up alongside of them and the driver motioned them into its dusty interior. Then, it rattled off with the two men ensconced inside. The engine appeared ready to die, but somehow it kept going. It reminded Thomas of the children's story—The Little Engine That Could.

I think I can! I think I can! The car seemed to be saying as it chugged along the deserted highway.

Two towns later, Thomas and Bob slid out of the passenger side of the car and into the street opposite a small café. It didn't look promising. It looked as if it was left over from a previous era when cowboys came to town and hung out at the nearest rooming house. Light could be seen through the old glass windows but the place appeared dreary and uninviting. As if by mutual agreement, they searched vainly for another restaurant. Then, gave up.

"Well, at least it's open," Thomas said.

"Yes, and I can guess what our Christmas dinner will be," Bob responded.

As they entered the café, Thomas saw four old men sitting in a corner, talking over some beers. Tom smelled the stale odor of cigarettes. An older woman stood behind the counter talking through a window separating the café from the kitchen. He could see the white hair and moustache of the cook.

The waitress was heavy-set with blond hair brushed back and held firmly in place by a thin red ribbon. Thomas looked around the café, but couldn't help thinking that this was no place for a dinner, least of all a holiday meal. The chairs and wooden tables were old and had a weather-beaten look to them. As he and Bob sat down at a nearby table, he could easily make out carved initials and words gouged into the tables. There was a wood burning stove giving off heat from a crackling fire.

In his mind's eye, Thomas visualized the snowy vistas of Bensenville at Christmas. The tree would be up at the Home and carols would be sung. There would be a church service and small gifts. He sighed and continued to sweep his eyes around the sparse cafe.

"Got a menu?" Bob asked.

"Yep." The waitress handed the two cadets well-worn paper menus, then pointed to a blackboard. "There's the specials."

She waited as they glanced down the menu.

"I'll have a hamburger," Thomas said. "Coffee and a piece of pie if you've got any." "Same here," Bob said.

"John, two burgers," she yelled. Then, she retreated behind the counter to get the coffee. When she returned, she held two steaming cups of coffee. Thomas took a quick swig. It tasted like chicory. Soon, hamburgers and fries arrived. As they sat in the nearly empty café, Thomas knew they were both thinking the same thing—what a Christmas!

◆   ◆   ◆

"You're wanted by the commandant," an aide notified Thomas several days after that meager Christmas meal.

He knew better than to ask, "Why?"

Thomas slowly put on his coat and headed out the barracks door toward the commandant's office. He knocked on the door and a gruff voice invited him in. Two officers were in the room. The commander was seated. A man who Thomas recognized as a senior flight trainer stood beside him.

"Thomas, we've been going through your papers and you are not the best pilot in the world," the commander said. "You are probably good enough to graduate, but more than likely you'll be a bomber pilot."

"Ever since I started to fly I wanted to be a fighter pilot," Thomas protested.

"No way. You don't do your spins good enough. Besides, you asked to be a navigator when you first began, didn't you?" the commander asked.

Thomas nodded.

"Well, we're really short of navigators and you're qualified."

He looked from one officer to the other. "But what about being a bomber pilot? he asked. The senior flight instructor snorted. "You'd never be satisfied. It's like flying a bus. You've felt the freedom of being in your own plane, handling it your own way. You'd feel hemmed in by the limits of a bomber."

Thomas felt as if his dreams of being a pilot had suddenly disappeared. Was this why he had dropped out of O.C.S.? He'd challenged the Army by just being here. Now what? He looked beyond the men to a map on the wall. He noticed that the Axis powers were marked in gray. Germany controlled Europe and Spain was neutral. On the other side of the map was the spreading menace of Japan. He'd volunteered to stop them. He'd put himself at risk. Why couldn't he be what he wanted to be—a pilot?

He refocused his attention on the flight instructor and commander. Did he want to continue and be a bomber pilot? No. They were right there. If he couldn't be a fighter pilot, than why not be a navigator? At least he would have control over directing a bomber on its runs.

The commander continued, "We'd like to send you to navigator school. We need navigators now. You can still be a pilot, but we are in desperate need of navigators."

Thomas felt the disappointment rising. But, he had to accept orders. There was no choice. If he couldn't be a good pilot, perhaps being a navigator might not be so bad.

"Where do I go?" And, when?"

"To San Antonio. As soon as possible. Here are your orders."

Thomas slowly reached out a hand and took the papers. He saluted and left the office, too stunned to think about how his position had changed in less than 15 minutes.

◆   ◆   ◆

San Antonio. A month-and-a-half more of waiting. During the time, Thomas again volunteered, this time to help run the supply room. Soon he was running the supply room. The officer-in-charge asked him if he wanted to stay there and run it permanently.

"I'll arrange to send you to O.C.S. and you can become a ground Air Force officer," he said.

"Thank you. But I volunteered to fight, not be in charge of supplies."

"You fly boys are all alike. You think the war can only be won in a plane. Providing supplies is just as important."

"I know they are important, sir. However, I want to be where the action is."

The officer shook his head and walked away.

So, he waited. He continued to help in the supply room but he also took advantage of opportunities to sneak into town. When he had initially been on the base at San Antonio, Thomas and some of the other cadets convinced the construction crew to leave a portion of the wire surrounding the base removable. All they had to do was unhook the wire like they would a fence, then go into the town itself. Thomas checked out the wire. The escape route was still there. A smile spread across his face. The waiting at San Antonio wasn't going to be so bad after all. He showed the fence to another man waiting for navigation school and the two of them found their way into town whenever they wanted.

Between volunteering to run the supply room and going into town, he kept busy. He received his orders to report to Houston for preliminary navigation school. This time no one was going to take this away. If he could, he'd be first in his class.

After processing, he met the captain of cadets, Roscoe Ates, a former movie star.

"What an arrogant, S.O.B.," Thomas said later. "He just reeks of his own importance."

"I know," another cadet responded. "I'd heard of him. But never believed someone could be that pompous."

Thomas became adjutant of cadets. He also began making friends. One of his best friends, Jerry Thaxton, became the cadet commander. One day Thomas received a letter from Marie. She wanted to come down for a visit on a weekend. It had been so long since he had seen her. He couldn't wait until she arrived.

Something unforeseen happened the day before she was scheduled to come. Those who had applied for leave had their leaves cancelled.

"You are all restricted to the base," the commander ordered.

"What's this about?" Thomas asked Jerry. He hadn't seen Marie in months. She was coming all the way from Chicago and he didn't want to lose a moment to some whim of the commander.

"Quiet, Thomas," Thaxton said. "He's about to tell us."

"We have the honor of having the First Lady visit us," the commander continued. "I want everyone in uniform and on hand when she arrives."

"I could care less about Eleanor Roosevelt," Thomas protested to the second in command. "My fiancée is in town."

"You heard the commander, Thomas. He wants everyone here. That means you."

Thomas turned on his heel and walked away. He'd have to get word to Marie.

When he was finally able to reach Marie by telephone, she seemed to understand. "Even if it's a short time, I want to see you," she said. "Mrs. Roosevelt can't be there all weekend."

"No, but she can wreck our portion of it," Thomas muttered. Even the privilege of going off base as cadet officers, couldn't take the sting off that lost weekend with Marie. They had so little time together before Marie had to return to

Chicago. Thomas tried to turn his attention elsewhere to get over the disappointment. Jerry seemed to understand his mood; he insisted that they take a Wednesday off so he could introduce Thomas to Galveston.

"Come on, Thomas, you haven't seen the best of Galveston unless you see the club I belong to and have a meal other than what the military offers."

Thomas readily agreed. They climbed into Thaxton's car and headed toward the seacoast. Jerry threaded his way through town and turned east. His club was located on the east side of Galveston. It had a back room for gambling that stretched out on a pier. The sound of thrown dice, the buzz of conversation and the smell of cigars could have drawn a blind man into the gambling arena. He enjoyed the club, but he was careful to keep his gambling to a minimum. The lure of the tables was too tempting for some. He was sure there were many who thought they could beat the house. He knew that was a losing proposition.

Thomas's trips to Galveston were short-lived. The moment he discovered Jerry Thaxton's club, he was sent to advanced navigation school at San Marcos. Instead of piloting the plane, he and other would-be navigators began flying missions where they practiced navigation. Each cadet learned to plot the position of the plane through every step of the flight.

At San Marcos, Thomas became friends with three other navigators—John E. "Knobby" Walsh, Lester Watts and Fred Wills. Wills and Thomas competed to be number one in their class. It was a friendly rivalry and out of it grew a strong friendship.

Thomas had had friends before, but the four of them were so close and did so many things together that other cadets began calling them the Four Horsemen. Wills got to be number one and Thomas became number two in their class. He didn't mind. He now had friendships that he believed would last a lifetime.

While at San Marcos, Thomas got a letter from Marie—"Let's get married," she wrote.

Thomas immediately called her, "If I can get permission, we'll go ahead. Early July okay?"

"Uh huh!"

◆   ◆   ◆

"What am I doing, Knobby? Is it right when we'll be shipping off so soon?"

"It's more right than you know." his friend replied. "Go get that permission."

A short time later Thomas came back to the barracks. "Well, I'm all set. When do you think it will happen to you, Knobby?"

Walsh looked away and didn't say anything.

Thomas stared at the firm face. The best lookin' guy I ever saw, he thought. Yet, it's as if he never wants to think about tomorrow. Well, if he doesn't, I must. I've got to get ready for that wedding.

Marie came down for the wedding the first week of July. They married July 3rd in the chapel on the base. Knobby Walsh was Thomas's best man. After the wedding, honeymooned in New Braunfels, the next town south of San Marcos. Thomas and Marie didn't even have a full week together, just two weekends. Then, Marie returned to Chicago.

After she left, Thomas graduated from navigation school and received his commission as a second lieutenant. He had no family to invite to pin his wings on. Marie couldn't come down again from Chicago, so he invited the Howell family, from Waco, to come to the graduation.

He asked Louise Howell to pin his wings on. She complied; kissing him lightly on the cheek like a mother would do to her son, while her husband, Hilton, shook his hand.

After receiving his wings, Thomas and the other graduates were granted two weeks leave. He made arrangements to join Marie in Chicago. After the two weeks, he'd report to Ephrata Air Base in Washington. He was another step closer to the fighting.

8

Journey to Britain

Chicago seemed so different during the war. When Thomas first arrived back in the city, he was struck by how many soldiers and sailors swarmed through the Loop area in the heart of the city. Small retail stores and larger ones clustered around State Street attracted the military. The Palmer House anchored one end of the thriving street and Marshall Fields the other. Across the Chicago River was the Gold Coast and Holy Name Cathedral.

There were few cars. He saw an occasional Hudson automobile. However, because of gasoline rationing, visitors and the military on leave in the City depended on public transportation. Those on leave referred to Chicago as Liberty Town. USO facilities were available. And jazz was a hot commodity in the many clubs in the downtown Loop, but Thomas spent most of his time with Marie. The two of them stayed with her parents before he left for the air base in Washington.

While he was in Chicago, he received a telephone call from Knobby Walsh's mother asking him about her son's whereabouts.

"He was supposed to be here for leave, Thomas. Do you know where he is? I'm beginning to worry."

Thomas knew Knobby was going to hitchhike to Chicago, but other than that, he had no specifics. "I think I know where he might be," he told Marie before coming back to the telephone. However, he wasn't going to let Mrs. Walsh into his thoughts.

"He should be home soon," he said. "Some of the navigators had to make up hours before coming home. That's probably what happened to Knobby."

He caught Marie's eye and silently shook his head.

"Well, if you think there's nothing to worry about?"

"Oh, I'm sure of that. Knobby knows how to take care of himself. When he gets here, Marie and I will stop by and visit you on the South Side."

He hung up and turned to Marie. "Knobby is probably having the time of his life," he said. "But go along with what I said, if she calls back."

"I think I know what you're thinking, Thomas. And, I can believe it of him."

A week later Knobby returned to Chicago. As promised, Thomas and Marie stopped by and visited the Walsh family. He also went to see his grandmother before returning to spend a last few days with Marie.

"Thomas, I will see you off with Marie when you return to duty," Grandmother Beyers said.

"I will be catching a train," Thomas said. "Are you sure you want to brave the crowds?"

His grandmother nodded.

After Thomas's grandmother and Marie accompanied him to the train for his trip to the airbase in Washington, he joined Knobby and Fred Wills in a compartment on the train.

"What happened to you Knobby?" Thomas asked when he had a chance to speak to him away from his South Side home. "Your mother called wanting to know where you were."

The dark-haired Walsh smiled, as if savoring a good memory. "What did you tell her Thomas?"

"Just that I thought you had to make up some hours in Texas before coming home."

"Good," he said. "You wouldn't believe what happened."

"Try me."

"Well, I hitch-hiked up to Dallas and got on a train to St. Louis," Knobby said and smiled again.

"Well you must have gotten to St. Louis. Then what?" Wills asked.

"Yes, I made it to St. Louis. While I was waiting for the train to Chicago, I decided to get a drink at a local bar." Knobby paused, before continuing, "There were these girls from a private college there."

"I see," Thomas said. He leaned slightly forward waiting for the Irishman to continue.

"It took me three days to get out of there," Knobby said.

Thomas sighed. He could imagine his friend buzzing around like a bee in a honeycomb.

"Then what?" Wills asked.

"Well, I got out of St. Louis and there was a stopover in Carbondale. Darned if the same thing didn't happen."

"Another girl's college?"

Knobby nodded. "This time it was Carbondale Teacher's College," he said.

Thomas met Wills' eyes; he could see that Fred didn't doubt the story in the least. Both knew that Knobby had a way with women, a way that they envied.

"You spent more time there?" Thomas asked. "Three days?"

Again, Knobby nodded. "It was a sweet time. Both were," Knobby concluded.

Thomas didn't press for any more details. He knew Knobby Walsh. If he ever wanted to tell him more about his experiences, he would.

In late October, the three of them arrived in Ephrata, Washington. Thomas took one look at the sky and wondered about wartime efficiency. Why were they sent to an area that looked as if it might have an early winter? As the clouds began closing in they brought snow.

One blustery November day as Thomas checked the bulletin board, he found a notice that those who were in the process of forming flight crews would be sent, by train, to Ardmore, Oklahoma.

"If I was in the air, this would have looked like a bunch of ants disappearing into toy trains," Thomas told Knobby as they queued up to catch the Oklahoma bound train.

"I think it would have been a little clearer than that," Knobby opined as he stood in line to board the steam-powered train.

Thomas and the other flight crews boarded the train and began the journey south, leaving behind the winter weather in Washington.

"It's going to take three or four days to get there, I bet we could make faster time if we hitchhiked," Knobby said.

"I'm sure we could," Thomas said. "But why report sooner than we have to just enjoy the trip down."

"It's not my idea of an enjoyable trip," Knobby protested.

On the trip south, Thomas noticed the men becoming more and more frustrated at the train's slow progress. He watched as a few of them gathered their belongings, determined to leave the laggard train behind and hitchhike to the Oklahoma base. At every stop in towns along the way, more of the men disappeared. When he and the others on board the train eventually reached Ardmore, the rest of their flight crews—gunners, radiomen and flight engineers—were waiting. He and Fred Will's crews were sent on to Rattlesnake Bomber Base in Pyote, Texas. It was the last stop before being sent overseas.

Pyote lay 22 miles east of Pecos. It was only a town of 340 people, windswept and covered with mesquite. The town was small and held several bars, a gas station and a store. The land where the base had been built once housed thousands of rattlesnakes. Dynamite had been used in an attempt to kill them off, but many snakes survived and continued to be a menace to the men on base. They would appear on the steps leading to the officers' mess or were encountered on the way to the latrines. As a precaution against the snakes, forty-five caliber side arms were distributed to the men.

"I thought the only reason we'd get guns was to fight the Jerries," Thomas said to one of his new crew. They were just beginning to get to know each other. Besides himself, there was the pilot, Roderick Steele; Thomas E. Fitzgerald, the bombardier; Robert Morrison, the radio man; and Edwin Marsh, Albert Grick, Dale Johnson, Robert Robinson and John Caum.

They flew training missions to New Orleans, Tennessee and Colorado. Thomas learned to navigate by the stars and by instruments, methodically plotting his way to their landings. Just as they reached the stage where they were about to leave for overseas, there was another delay. Steele, their pilot, decided he didn't want to fly any more.

"I don't want the responsibility, Thomas. I know the men. If it comes right down to it, I don't want their lives on my conscience."

"All of us have each other's lives on our hands, Rod," Thomas said. "If the gunner misses, we can get shot down. If I don't get us to the right target, we could end up bombing an area that we shouldn't. And, what if I miscalculate our flight to a base? Don't you think I worry about that?"

"Yes, but in a different way."

"Is it so different?"

"You have a calmness, a determination. You aren't afraid to take a chance, Thomas. I don't want the others to be killed if I fail."

"Roderick…"

"It's no use, Thomas. I'm asking to be relieved."

"You're under-estimating yourself."

"Well, it's done."

So, he and the others waited for a new pilot. While they waited, Steele remained on the base. Thomas could see his uncertainty every time Roderick looked at the crew. Finally, after the new pilot, Jerry T. Musser, arrived, Steele asked to be reinstated as a copilot.

"I don't mind flying, but I don't want the responsibility of the crew," he said.

"That's too bad, Roderick," Thomas said. "You're a damn good pilot. You shouldn't be a second officer."

◆   ◆   ◆

Time no longer dragged by for the new crew. Thomas wrote more often to Marie, knowing that he would soon have to leave the country for his tour overseas. It was early December and Marie wrote him that she wanted to visit him at the base in Pyote. He readily agreed. They had had so little time together since they had married and he longed to see her.

Marie left Chicago on December 19. It took a day for her to reach Pyote and Thomas arranged for her to stay in the Texas Hotel in Monahans, Texas, the next town to the east of Pyote. Monahans was larger than the small town where the base was located and he looked forward to every minute he could spend with her.

While she was there, he was ordered to take his final physical examination before going overseas.

"Just another in the long list of government procedures," Thomas told her as he went to the base after spending the evening together.

After the exam, the physician called him into his office.

"Thomas, we'll have to ground you," the doctor said. "You've got a deviated septum."

"A what?"

"A deviated septum. It's when your nasal cavity is off center. The wall between the left and right sides of your nose should be centered. Your nasal wall is not. One side of your nose is wider than the other and it blocks the normal airflow. It affects your breathing. Because it affects breathing, you can't fly at high altitudes."

"I've been flying."

"I know. You shouldn't have been."

"Isn't there a way to get around this?" Thomas asked. "I want to be a part of this war effort. I don't want to let the crew down."

The physician hesitated. "Well, you could have an operation. The septum can be moved to a normal position so your breathing is not affected and the airflow is equal between both nostrils. Are you sure you want to go through it?"

Without hesitation, Thomas answered, "Yes!"

"We'll have to schedule it for tomorrow."

"Fine. That will give me time to tell my wife. She's here from Chicago."

"That could be an advantage for you. She can look after you while you mend."

As Thomas left the office to tell Marie, he heard the physician arranging for the procedure to take place. He gave little thought to what the doctors would do.

Instead, he thought of being able to continue with his objective of serving over-seas as a navigator.

When he saw Marie that evening, he explained what the doctors would do.

"Thomas, I was going to go back to Chicago tomorrow. There's no way I will leave at a time like this," she said. "Are you sure you want to do this?" she asked. Her concern showed on her face and in her voice.

"I'm sure Marie. It's the only way I'll be able to be a part of the crew and to serve my country in the way I've been trained."

"Very well," Marie said. "I'll call my mother and tell her. She'll inform the manager at Sears I'll be delayed in returning."

The following day he reported to the medical facility for the operation. He was led into a small operating room. There, he saw a high-backed chair and nearby a table with a tray containing scalpels, and other medical equipment.

"Sit in this chair, Thomas, and we'll get to work," the physician ordered.

Thomas watched with some trepidation as the doctor reached for a syringe to deaden the skin and nerves around his nose and mouth. The physician and his assistant then put cotton in to stop the drainage of blood into his sinuses.

Thomas sat, aware of what was happening, yet only able to sit and watch. He saw the white-gloved hand of the doctor reach for what looked like a miniature saw.

Oh no, Thomas thought. What have I gotten myself into? He watched the man approach him with the blade and heard the doctor attacking the partition separating the two cavities in his nose. It was soon over. The physician staunched the blood that was trickling down his nose and covered it with gauze.

"You'll be fine, Thomas," the doctor said. "Just take it easy. This will take a few days to heal and you can join your unit."

The following day Thomas felt the pain from the operation. And, he began to wonder if it was worth it. Marie attempted to feed him and touched his lip slightly. The agony from her light touch was almost more than he could bear. She continued to watched over him, staying until New Year's Day.

Just before she was about to leave, he received his orders to report to Kearney, Nebraska, and was given five days leave. He could return to Chicago with Marie.

Marie checked out of the Texas Hotel and joined Thomas, Rod Steele and Fitzgerald, the bombardier, in catching a ride to Fort Worth. From there, they took a train back to Chicago.

Thomas again spent as much time as he could with Marie while they stayed at her mother's house on the northwest side of Chicago. The two women accompa-nied him to the train for his journey to Nebraska. As he boarded the train, he wondered when he would see them again. It would certainly not be before the war ended. He waved goodbye and the train steamed out.

At Kearney he joined his crew and completed their orders to pick up their new 75 foot long B17. Thomas stood silently eyeing the plane that they would fly overseas. He estimated the bomber's height as nearly 20 feet. The four engines were evenly spaced out on the left and right side of the crew's quarters.

"This baby's got wings 103 feet, nine inches long," Musser said.

Thomas climbed into the plane's nose section. The navigator's wooden desk and chair sat just beneath a machine gun. Thomas had concentrated on learning how to navigate the plane. He knew that after his duties as navigator were fulfilled, he would be expected to man the machine gun above him. He and the bombardier were in the farthest forward compartment with the bombardier's controls and twin nose guns in a power turret. Above and behind them was the flight deck, where Roderick Steele and the new pilot handled the flight controls of the plane.

The compartments of the plane from the tail gunner to the nose section were connected. However, the passages between the areas were extremely narrow. This was especially true of the eight-inch catwalk that connected the front section of the plane to the bomb bay and on through to the radio operator's station. Thomas hoped he would never have to thread through the plane to the tail gunner's section. At least there was more than one emergency exit from the plane, he thought, as his eyes drifted over the plane from the tail section to the bubble area where he and the bombardier's quarters were in the nose.

◆   ◆   ◆

After picking up the new plane, the crew again practiced missions to become familiar with the bomber. In the first part of January 1944, they took off for Europe. They stopped in Maine to pick up fuel, waited a day, and then took off for Goose Bay, Labrador.

My first trip outside the country, Thomas thought. I'd better get us there okay. He checked and double-checked his calculations as they took off. Their first leg of the journey to the war in Europe had begun.

It began to snow as they put down in Labrador. When Thomas and the others climbed out of the plane, he saw a hockey rink close to the base. It was clearly visible to the crew and Thomas unconsciously marked its height and location. It continued to snow for two days and stopped. When he looked for the rink again, it had completely disappeared. The new snow covered it so thoroughly that any new planes coming in would not even know it was there. That night the crew learned another storm was heading their way. They received orders to take off before the storm struck.

"Normally you'd fly to Greenland, then to Iceland, then down to Scotland. But we want to see if its feasible to take a direct route to Ireland and then to England," they were told. "We want to get as many planes out before the weather makes it impossible to take off."

The crew boarded their flight and warmed up the engines. As they did, the snow started to fall again. Thomas's plane and two other aircraft got off the ground and headed east. Behind them, the storm hit and began to cover the base like a blanket.

"They've closed the base," Steele said from the cockpit. "We have to outrun this storm as we head east."

On the way over, they flew above the clouds and the only thing that Thomas could use for navigation was the sun. Every 15 minutes he took a reading with his sextant.

The readings show where we are east and west, but not north and south, he thought. If I could only see the ocean, I could plot our position with more certainty by looking at the waves. Thomas knew that if the waves were blowing a certain way and depending on their height he could estimate the strength of the wind. He looked down at the clouds trying to get a glimpse of the ocean again. If only there was an opening in the clouds, he could tell whether they were off course.

"Can't see a damn thing down there," he muttered. They would have to depend on the readings from the sun and hope his estimation of arrival time was correct.

The hours went by and he could feel the wind buffeting the plane. As they approached Ireland, Thomas felt confident that he'd plotted their route perfectly. Yet, when he looked out to confirm they were over the Irish coast, he saw no land. Clouds surrounded them and neither land nor ocean were visible. He wondered, Could I have possibly miscalculated?

Thomas couldn't help but think of the saying, "There's no room in a lifeboat for a navigator." When would the coast come into view?

"The wind must be affecting us," he told the pilot. "I think we're over Ireland but I don't have any way of verifying it."

The pilot took the plane down several thousand feet. Cloud cover was almost complete, but finally there was a break in the clouds and the crew could see land. However, the time of arrival was 10 minutes off what Thomas had estimated.

Since they had no heading for the airport, the pilot put out a call to the Royal Air Force (RAF) to guide them to their destination.

A few minutes later Rod Steele interrupted his worries about whether he had been correct in his first big test as a navigator.

"Relax Thomas, they're sending up a fighter to guide us down," said Steele. "You did a good job. We're right where we're supposed to be."

The fighter came along side, wagged its wings, and then spurted ahead of them. Musser positioned the plane directly behind the RAF aircraft and followed it into the base at Nuts Corner, Ireland. After spending a day-and-a-half in Ireland, Thomas, Steele and the new pilot got back on board the plane and flew over to London, dropping the plane off at Bovington, where it would be upgraded to combat readiness. The rest of the crew joined them and they learned they were assigned to the 96th Bomb Group at Snetterton Heath, in East Anglia, England.

Before leaving for their new base, the pilots were given additional training in a flight simulator. While the pilots trained, Thomas spent five days of that first week in London learning the latest navigation systems. The new system used radio signals transmitted from three different stations and picked up on a device similar to a radar. The British and American crews called it the Gee Box. After their training, the entire crew was transferred to Snetterton Heath.

The moment that Thomas had awaited since he first volunteered to be an Army Air Corps cadet was upon him. Almost two years had passed, but he was now part of the war effort, just like his brothers. William, his older brother, had joined the Army. Thomas wasn't certain where he was stationed. Fred, the youngest, a marine, was captured at Corregidor and was a prisoner of the Japanese. Richard, who had been so close to Thomas at Bensenville, had joined the Air Force too and was stationed in the States.

God willing, we'll all live through the war and meet back in Chicago, Thomas thought.

9

Milk Runs

After a week of flying practice runs all over England, Thomas and his crew were judged ready to become a part of the air war against Germany. No longer would he be practicing navigation and learning the countryside of England. The time for waiting was past. He and the crew were now a part of the 96th Air Group, a part of the 8th Air Force stationed at Snetterton Heath in East Anglia.

The rural area of Snetterton spread out for miles. It reminded Thomas of the description of the English countryside he had read about in the Sherlock Holmes books of his youth. The nearest small town to the base was Attleborough. The closest village, Eccles, bordered the base and a railroad bisected the base. The flying area housing the planes and runway lay to the west of the rail line, while the living area, mess hall and officer's club was on the east.

Thomas had flown practice runs out of Snetterton prior to entering the combat theater. However, his baptism of fire officially began March 26, 1944. The crew's first "milk-run" was a quick flight over the Cherbourg peninsula, on the coast of France. Although it was considered a milk run, the 20 planes that hit the coast still struck an important target, the V-weapon site at Mesnil Au Val.

The so-called milk runs introduced Thomas to the reality of war. As he peered down at the coast, he became aware of the covert and anonymous nature of war. Below him were weapons of mass destruction, hidden on the coast, but ready to take off and destroy sectors of London.

Further inland lay the airfields that housed the German Luftwaffe. He was not anxious to meet other planes in aerial combat. That time would come later. Meanwhile, he hoped that their attack was successful. But, he would only know if there were fewer attacks on England from this location.

The milk-run flights did not have the danger of later flights. However, the crews received a taste of their role in aerial combat. The flights also served a purpose. Unlike other planes that had adopted a name for their bomber, the crew of the B-17G had a number and no name. This seemed to suit the nature of this war. It was an impersonal attack of one force against another.

Before taking off, he and the crew had been briefed on how the German Luftwaffe attacked the flying fortresses.

"They fly parallel to the plane's stream, but out of range of the guns," said a briefing officer. "Then, they turn ahead of the leader and come straight at you."

"What can we do?" one of the pilots asked.

"Nothing, the only thing that helps is if one of our own fighter pilots gets them first."

Thomas and his crew left the debriefing aware for the first time of the weaknesses of the vaunted bomber. It was not like a castle with soldiers ready and able to repel all attacks. The bombers were vulnerable, much more than he had ever known.

As he sat at the wooden desk in the plane's nose, plotting the attack, Thomas could feel the tension of the other crewmembers. For them the real war was about to begin. He looked up at the bombardier who was further forward in the nose and to his right. Fitzgerald raised a thumbs up, before turning his head toward the Plexiglas window to keep an eye out for fighters. Twenty-one planes had taken off that morning. Only one plane had to abort. They reached their target and Thomas saw a burst of enemy fire exploding close to the other planes.

That must be flak, he thought. He watched as the deadly barrage stitched a pattern across parts of the morning sky. Thomas viewed it with fascination. It will never hit us, he thought, as he watched it. Yet, the flash of light, the tracers going across the sky and the rumble of explosions buffeting the plane caused him to wonder if enemy planes were near. He searched the sky for the dreaded German fighters and was thankful he didn't see any.

This time the planes returned safely after dumping their bombs. He and the crew disembarked from the plane without a word. The attack had been quick. He looked around to make sure the other planes had returned safely and breathed a sigh of relief. All of the planes had returned. He knew this wouldn't always be the case. Yet, for his first venture into combat, it was comforting.

On March 28, another "milk run" was assigned. This time the target was Château din, France. On the first mission to the coast, the boxed barrage that blanketed certain sections of the sky appeared sparse. Thomas detected a feeling of confidence among the pilots and crews that the war was beginning to turn in the Allies direction.

Were they too confident? Or, was this only a faint promise of what might be? Eventually there would come a time when the Allies would invade the continent.

He hoped that that invasion would be soon. He'd only been in England a short time, but like the other pilots he wanted to finish the war and return home.

Thomas was under no illusions during the second "milk run." He knew that when they flew further into Europe the difficulties in coming back alive would increase. There would be German fighters further inland. Then the crews would see more flak and face enemy fighters protecting the interior. Once again, all planes returned safely to the base at Snetterton.

The base held over 3,000 personnel. Of these personnel, 545 men were on some form of flight status. Despite their numbers, the continuous bombing of Europe exacted a heavy toll from the aviators. New crews and planes were constantly brought in to replace planes lost to enemy fire. Thomas heard that more than two-thirds of American aviators had not finished their tours of 25 missions in 1943.

On their third mission, Thomas's squadron struck Germany. The intense flak was like nothing he'd ever seen. He wondered how they could return to base without anyone missing. But, they did. After this mission, he and several of the crew went to a party on April 1. It was the 100th Mission Party and among the guests were Lt. General James H. Doolittle and Sir Arthur Harris, Air Chief Marshal and commanding officer of the RAF Bomber Command. Doolittle had led the first attack against the Japanese home islands in 1942. The general had been a Lt. Colonel at that time. Now he commanded the Eighth Air Force in England. Thomas had seen Doolittle's picture in the papers. However, here at the party, he seemed more the picture of a studious professor than a general.

Liquor flowed as heavily as speeches. Officers and crews concentrated on enjoying themselves. Thomas went over to the bar to get a drink. While waiting, he could see and hear the bespectacled Doolittle discussing the objectives of the war.

"We must take control of the skies over Europe," the General said.

"Agreed," said Harris. "That will help in the coming land offensive."

"Yes, and it will shorten the war." said Ira C. Eaker, another general at the festivities. "The Germans are still a threat to our planes."

No news there, Thomas thought. He ordered a beer.

"Yes, but we're shooting more of their fighters down all the time. When they ignore our fighters and come up and attack the bombers, that's when we eliminate them," Doolittle said. "I'd be willing to trade one bomber for each fighter to eliminate the German Luftwaffe."

Thomas and the men around him looked sharply at the general. He could feel the flight officers' anger, but he recognized the general's point. They needed to establish air supremacy. However, he didn't need to say he'd trade ten men in a bomber for one man in a fighter. This was not the time or place to make such a statement. He grabbed his beer, turned on his heel and walked away. Like many other airmen, he was relieved he didn't have to fly immediately after the bash. Whether it was bad weather or the party, it was a week before the crews ventured back into Germany.

◆   ◆   ◆

Thomas had always awakened early at the Home in Illinois and during training in the Army Air Corps. However, he had not had to awaken at 4 a.m. to dress, eat breakfast and be briefed on the targets of the day. He soon adjusted to the early morning wakeups and fell into the required routine before the day's flight.

On April 9, the crews were briefed that they would take part in a raid into Posen, Poland and Rostock, Germany. The weather over England was bad when they took off. As they climbed into the clouds, Thomas wondered if the planes would be called back.

The flight to Posen would take them deep into Europe, but they were to take a different approach to the bombing. The bombers flew into Poland from the north rather than directly across the Channel, the shortest route to the target. Still wondering about the viability of the raid, he looked out the window. It appeared as if some of the planes had peeled off and returned to base.

"Any word about turning back, Thomas?" the bombardier asked.

Thomas shook his head.

"What about this new pilot they assigned us?"

"Don't know anything about him either, Fitz. All I know is he's near the end of his 25 missions."

"Well, he must have plenty of experience then."

Thomas nodded. He didn't know him but he appeared to be a better pilot than the one who'd flown over to England with the crew. However, he seemed distant. Maybe that was what happened the closer you got to the end of your tour of duty.

"It seems like there's less planes in the group. If they've turned back, why don't we get any word?" Fitzgerald asked.

Again, Thomas said nothing. The flight was longer coming in from the north and he wondered how much of the target would be visible through the heavy clouds. Then, the clouds opened and he saw Posen below.

Just as he was able to see the target plainly, it appeared the gunners on the ground could see them clearly. It seemed as if every flak gun across Europe was trained on their plane. Flak hit the plane blowing out the Plexiglas in the plane's nose and causing damage to the electrical system. Thomas could also tell that there was also damage to the wing by the way the plane was reacting. After hitting the target, they retraced their steps to England. On the way back fighters attacked the plane as it crossed the Baltic Sea.

"Captain, I can plot a course to Sweden," Thomas said through his radio.

"No, we're going back to England," the captain informed him.

"But half the electrical system is out," Thomas said. He could feel the cold creeping into the plane.

"We're flying to England. I'm almost at the end of my 25 missions. I don't want to be interned until the war is over."

"An engine's out," the bombardier called out.

"Yes, and we're just south of Sweden," Thomas said. A little later, he radioed the pilot, "We're over the North Sea, Captain,"

Thomas looked at the bombardier who just shook his head. 25,000 feet up, he thought as he fingered his gloves. There was no warmth to them. When the electrical system went, the heat for his electrical gloves went too. He clenched his teeth as he felt the cold coming through. There was no choice. He had to remove his gloves to plot the course back to the base.

"If we crash in the North Sea, we won't last 15 minutes," Thomas muttered. He took fixes with the Gee Box on his position every few minutes, all the while feeling the numbing effect of the cold on his exposed fingers. He put his gloves on trying to find any semblance of warmth. Useless. His fingers were really beginning to hurt. He caught the eye of the bombardier who sat watching him. Was he reading sympathy in his face? Or, was there only one thought in his mind, safety?

They crossed the North Sea. He looked at his fingers. They were turning blue. Can't do anything about them, he thought. He concentrated on the course and finally heard the captain say, "We'll make an emergency landing on the eastern coast. Get rid of our heavy equipment. Throw it over board."

Thomas and the crewmembers scrambled to throw out everything they could. The pilot was having difficulty keeping the plane level as the men methodically rid the plane of extra weight. When he returned to his position at the navigation desk, he looked at the bombardier and then toward the heavy machine guns.

"They won't do us any good if we're in the drink," Thomas said. The bombardier agreed. Both of them grasped the guns and jettisoned them through the damaged nose of the plane. There was nothing left to get rid of. Now all they could do was wait. He heard the distant words of the bombardier, "Why risk everybody's lives to get back because our pilot is near the end of his flight tour? He could have gotten us killed."

Thomas agreed. But, his hands hurt too much to say anything.

"Thank God," he whispered as he felt the plane beginning its descent. Thomas put his hands back in his gloves. His work was done. They'd made it. After they landed, he noticed his fingers were slowly turning from blue to white. He shivered. He could feel pain and suspected that he had frostbite.

The crewmembers on the flight back to base had been subdued. Death had come too close to them. The sky that appeared non-threatening now looked as if it was waiting to uncloak the dangers that were all too real in the war. The men did not want to think about their buddies who had been shot down. Instead, Thomas and the others longed for the safety of Snetterton. When he got back to the base, he slowly disembarked walking past the pilot without a word.

At the base, Thomas learned that one of the pilots on another plane had been wounded. He knew the injured pilot so when he and Fred Wills had an opportunity they went to visit him in the hospital.

"How is he, Doc?" Thomas asked.

"He'll be fine. His wound will heal and he'll be sent home."

Thomas and Fred entered the room where the pilot lay in bed.

"You've got it made, buddy," Thomas said as he greeted him. "You're going to be okay. You'll be sent home."

"Yeah. Sure."

The pilot looked away, staring at a bare wall nearby. He lay there, with no expression. It didn't seem like he was even aware that Fred and Thomas were there.

"Well, maybe we'd better let you rest. We'll be back tomorrow," Thomas said.

When they returned the next day, Thomas found out that the pilot had died during the night.

"I don't understand, Doc. You said he'd be fine," Thomas said.

"He should have been," the doctor responded. "There was no reason for him to die. He just gave up."

"But why?"

"That's what I've been asking myself," the surgeon said. His blood shot eyes indicated the man had slept little. He had no explanation for the pilot's death. Idly, he reached over to a crumpled up letter in the room.

"Maybe this explains it," he said after reading it. He gave it to Thomas.

As Thomas read it, he looked up at the surgeon and then to Wills.

"What is it Thomas?" Wills asked.

"It's a Dear John letter, Fred."

"Damn. So, that's why."

Thomas nodded and gave the letter back to the surgeon. "I think you're right," he said. "I think he did give up after getting that."

They left the room and returned to the base at Snetterton. Better to think of completing his tour of duty and returning home, Thomas thought. Don't think of that pilot. Think of other things.

Other flights followed to Florennes, Belgium and Rostock, Germany. Again, flak was heavy. Thomas saw fighters swoop into the flight lanes ahead of other planes, speed toward them, shooting 20-mm cannon shells. He watched as plane after plane was attacked, blew up or went down like a screaming hawk with little or no time for the airmen on board to parachute. Others got out of their planes, only to be hit by debris from other doomed planes. Still, there were survivors. He saw some of the parachutes open, clear of the burning sky above and float down with living persons hanging from the umbrella-shaped chutes.

A few days later Fred and Thomas decided to visit Knobby Walsh at the 94th Bomb Group at Bury St. Edmunds. It would do them both good. Knobby had a way of making things brighter and less threatening. He insisted on living for the present. Perhaps that was the key to survival.

On April 17, the three navigators got together at Walsh's base. It was a good time. Thomas was thankful he had stopped to see him. They talked of old times as they sipped a warm English beer. Yet, his friend from Chicago still acted as if he was living on borrowed time.

Fred and Thomas returned to the 96th Air Group at Snetterton that night. They were scheduled to fly on the 18th and hit Luneberg Germany's Luftwaffe installations. When Thomas returned to base after the raid, he learned Walsh's plane had been shot down.

"Maybe he was taken prisoner," Thomas said when Fred Wills told him.

"You know that didn't happen, Thomas."

"I don't want to believe he's gone until it's confirmed," Thomas stated. Yet, he was almost as sure of Knobby's fate as Fred. There was something about the way Knobby knew he wouldn't survive the war.

Thomas, Roderick Steele and a buddy, Carl Clark, received a 24-hour pass after a raid on Lipstadt, Germany.

They opted to see London. Clark left them half way through the pass and Steele and Thomas made their way to the Grovesnor's Hotel. As they entered the old hotel that had been turned into an allied officer's club, they decided to have tea. They were sitting, relaxing, when two young women approached them and asked if they could join them.

They must be near 18, Thomas thought. The one had striking, brown hair, cut short and she was dressed in the khaki uniform of the British Wrens. The other woman, who also was dressed in the British Wrens uniform, seemed to defer to the slim brown-haired woman.

"Do you come here often?" the young woman with short brown hair asked.

"This is our first time," Thomas answered. He looked around the old hotel, thinking it must have really been something during peacetime. His attention returned to the women who had joined them.

"You're Yanks," the brown-haired woman said. It wasn't a question, but a statement.

"Yes, miss," he said. "What is your name?"

"Elizabeth," she answered.

"How long have you been in the Wrens?" Thomas asked.

"Oh, just about a year. We both drive lorries," Elizabeth answered as she sipped her tea. The other woman looked at her watch. "We'd best get back," she said.

Elizabeth nodded. Standing, she looked back at Rod and Thomas. "We'll see you again."

After they left, a British officer approached. "Do you know who you were talking to?" he asked.

Thomas shook his head. All he knew was the woman appeared young and pleasant.

"That was Princess Elizabeth."

Princess Elizabeth? Thomas thought. But his reaction to the news was the same as his friend, Rod.

"So what!" Rod and Thomas said together.

"Bloody Yanks!" the officer stammered, turned on his heel and left.

Thomas, an Army Air Corps cadet in 1942.

Almost Airborne.
Thomas attends flight school as a flying cadet in Sweetwater, Texas

"The Four Horsemen" (left to right)
Les Watts, Tom Thomas, Fred Wills and John "Knobby" Walsh at Navigation School, San Marcos, Texas.

The crew of "The Chief"—FIRST ROW (left to right), Harold L. Nis-wonger (pilot), Roderick B. Steele (copilot), Thomas L. Thomas (navigator and Thomas E. Fitzgerald (bombardier). SECOND ROW—Robert R. Robinson (tail gunner), Robert J. Morrison (radio operator), John R. Caum (engineer), Edwin H. March (ball turret gunner), Albert Grick (right waist gunner) and Dale J. Johnson (left waist gunner).

Control Tower, 96th Bomb Group at Snetterton-Heath, England, 1944.

Bombers on the attack over Germany.

The wallet that saved a life.

MAY 8, 1944

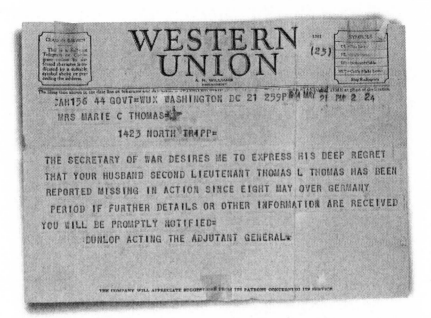

Western Union Telegram
notifies Marie that Thomas is missing in action, May 21, 1944.

Marie, summer 1944, when Thomas was a prisoner.

Prison camp, West Compound, Sagan.

A barracks room building in Sagan Luft III.

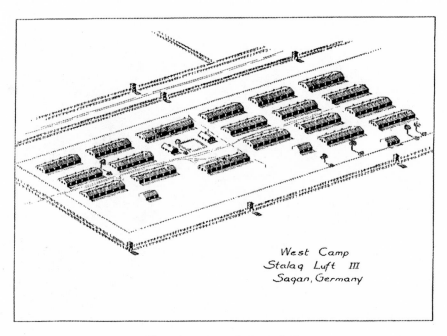

The prison camp, Stalag Luft III.

The blizzard march in January 1945.

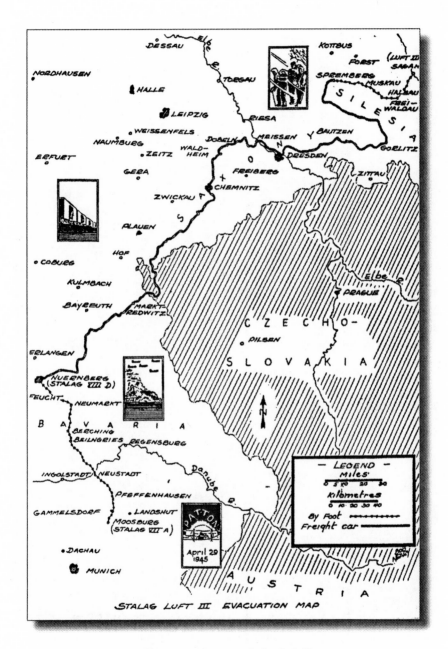

The evacuation map, Stalag Luft III

Barracks at Moosberg day after liberation, April 29, 1945.

Camp Lucky Strike near LeHavre, France.

10

Part of the Action

After their return from London, Thomas and the crew were assigned another veteran pilot for a raid, April 24th, on Friedrickshaven, Germany. The city shared a lake with Switzerland. It was hard to imagine that on one side of an invisible boundary lay a neutral nation. On the other side lay a country that had invaded and conquered much of Europe. Beneath them was the German city with aircraft factories and submarine manufacturing and testing facilities nearby. Frederickshaven only appeared peaceful for a short time. His plane joined 17 other planes as they began their bombing runs on the city.

Thomas had little time to admire the view above the urban center. Flak was heavy. He'd heard other fliers describe the flak as being as thick as dirty cotton and he had to agree. Not only was it thick, it seemed unerringly accurate. He felt the plane shudder as it continued on to the target.

"We've been hit," Thomas said. He glanced at the bombardier who was getting ready to release the bombs.

Come on. Come on. Let's get out of here, he thought. But, it was the bombardier's plane now. He controlled the approach and release of the bombs. Finally, the bombs dropped and the plane continued on its course until the pilot resumed control and began evasive action.

Thomas felt the plane bank for its return to England. The evasive action seemed to come too late. He felt the plane shudder, as if a giant hand had taken it within its grasp and shaken it.

"An engine's out," someone called out.

Thomas could smell the smoke from the engine. He watched anxiously until the pilot feathered it. They were still air borne, but they were beginning to lose altitude. He looked over the shoulder of the bombardier. They were falling behind the other planes in the squadron. If this continued, they'd be sitting ducks for any German fighters in the area.

"Captain, do you want me to plot a course to Switzerland?" Thomas called over the intercom.

"Negative."

"Another 25 mission guy," Fitzgerald muttered.

"You forget, Fitz. It's now 30 missions."

Thomas met the bombardier's eyes. He knew they were both thinking of the flight to Posen that had almost cost them their lives. Unconsciously, he rubbed his hands together. Although their electrical system was still functional, it was as if the memory of that flight was causing his hands to grow cold again.

"We're really shot up," Fitzgerald said as he looked toward the engine that no longer functioned. Both men saw the pepper-like wounds that spread along the wing like the tracks of a stray bird, scratching its talons into the steel on one end of the wing and moving toward the enclosure that housed the crew. He and Fitzgerald looked at the other wing.

"A matched pair, except for the engine," Thomas said. He glanced toward his navigation tools. What he wouldn't give to be out of the sky and safe in Switzerland.

Why did this guy have to get back to England? He wanted to go home too, but he wouldn't have risked the lives of the men in the plane.

The sky was too blue. Their plane was too visible to the artillery beneath them, Thomas thought. Flak continued to pepper the sky around them. Amazingly, they were still flying. All the crew could do was sit back and hope that the pilot made it.

As Thomas looked into the afternoon sun, he strained to catch sight of any German fighters that might be approaching. He didn't see any. He turned back to his desk and concentrated on plotting a course back to Snetterton. After recording their position in his log, he looked down on a forest and a road leading out of it.

"That's strange," he said. "There's a paved road leading into that forest."

"So?" Fitz asked. "A lot of times there's paved roads going into forests."

"This is different," Thomas said. He kept staring at the road and the forest. He marked the coordinates to pass on after the flight. And, he continued to stare at the road.

"There. Did you see that?"

"What?"

"I think I saw a plane on that road."

Fitzgerald leaned over and looked toward the forest. "I don't see a thing. Are you sure?"

"Positive. I've taken down the coordinates. When we get back I'll report it," He shifted his attention back to their situation and the flight to Snetterton.

Every so often, there would be a rumble like thunder bursting around them. Thomas would brace himself and glance at the flak. The German artillery continued to fire shells at the retreating B-17s as they headed toward the Channel. Perhaps they would make it. Perhaps fate hadn't gotten their number after all.

"Maybe we'll get another pilot who gives a damn about his crew," Fitz said as he broke into Thomas's thoughts.

"I hope so," Thomas agreed. He was amazed they had even made it to the Channel. The ice-cold sea took longer to cross retreating then attacking. He breathed a sigh of relief when he saw the coastline ahead of them. They started their descent. Thomas saw the water beneath them as they flew toward shore. It looked as if they were only 100 feet above it.

"I wonder how much fuel we lost when that engine was destroyed," Thomas whispered.

Fitzgerald turned and looked at him. His face no longer revealed anger at the pilot. Now his face reflected the worry that Thomas felt. Would their fuel last? Could they land safely?

"Sorry, Fitz. I shouldn't have said that," Thomas said. He couldn't take back the words. He'd voiced his own fears and now the bombardier was looking toward the feathered engine.

"You think we have enough in the tank, Thomas?"

"I hope so. There's been no word from Steele or the pilot about bracing for a landing. So, maybe that's good news."

Thomas forced himself to check his maps, hoping that they were close enough to the base. Then, he felt the wheels touch ground. As they landed, the other engine stopped.

Fitzgerald rose and faced Thomas. "We can't continue to have this type of luck," he said. "Somewhere, sometime it'll catch up to us."

The words might be true, but neither man could afford to think that way. If they did, it might be like a self-fulfilling prophecy. Thomas stopped the bombardier. "We control the luck. Let's not put it outside our control," he said. "I don't want any doubt about our going back home to enter the picture. Understand?"

The bombardier nodded.

They could control much of their future. Yet, if they were to survive they had to have someone else pilot them. Neither said another word. They had flown with each other long enough to know when there was agreement on the question of survival.

The crew dragged themselves to the debriefing and Thomas mentioned seeing a road and what he thought was a plane on the road coming out of the forest. He gave the coordinates to the officer in charge.

"We'll send a scout plane in and check it out Thomas," the interrogation officer said as Thomas left to return to his barracks.

◆   ◆   ◆

The next day, April 25, brought another flight, this time to Dijon, France. That day also brought another pilot, Harold Niswonger.

Niswonger was part German and part American Indian. Thomas and the crew immediately took to their new leader. They liked his steadiness. He was a skilled pilot. It showed on the flight to Dijon. He methodically did his job, turned the plane around and returned to base.

"This guy isn't out for his 30th mission," said Fitz.

"No, maybe with him we'll make it through to our 30th."

"You know, if it works out Thomas, why don't we give our plane a name like so many others have? Why not 'The Chief?'"

"Good idea," Thomas said. For the first time in days, he and the bombardier exchanged smiles as they left the plane. Even the copilot, Steele, seemed at ease.

Four days later, on April 29, the crew received a briefing for their next target—Brunswick. Again, there was little or no fighter opposition to the attack. There was supposed to be a stand down on the evening of May 7th. Thomas was in a mood to relax. He went over to the officer's club and saw no indication they were to fly the next day. Like many of the others on base, he decided to have a few drinks. He left the club about 1 a.m., feeling relaxed and at ease with the world.

"I'm drunk," Thomas whispered. His head was beginning to hurt. After he left the club, others remained enjoying drinks and talking. It was the only relief they had from the stress of flying into the enemy's backyard. He walked unsteadily back to the barracks and sprawled out on his bed. It would be nice to sleep late, he thought before dozing off.

Roderick Steele came into the barracks and shook him awake at 4 a.m. the following morning. Bleary-eyed, Thomas opened one eye. This couldn't be happening. There was no reason to get up at this hour.

"Come on Thomas," Steele said. "They called off the stand down."

"They can't do that," Thomas objected. "No one from the 96th will be sober enough to fly."

"You underestimate our ability to hold liquor," Steele laughed.

Thomas pulled on his shoes and followed the copilot toward the door. He hadn't bothered to undress the night before. So, he wouldn't be the most presentable officer attending briefing. However, he suspected everyone would be in the same shape. He sat well to the back as the briefing began.

"We are going to Berlin today," the officer began. Maps were projected on the screen showing the targets. The bombing by the Allies had become a 24-hour siege. Thomas and the others were a part of the siege. He tried not to think of the lives his plane had ended. If he was to retain his sanity in this hellish war, he could only think of shortening the war by hitting military targets. But every so often, he heard of the cost of civilian lives.

Thank God he hadn't been a part of the Anglo-American attack on Berlin in March. He had heard that attack had killed thousands of civilians. Then, there was Hamburg. How many had died there?

An officer called Thomas over as the crews were about to leave for their planes.

"Well done, Thomas. What you saw on the raid to Friedrickshaven was an airplane factory."

"It was?" Thomas tried to concentrate on the officer's words.

"Yes, it was. We confirmed your sighting and bombed the hell out of it." He reached over and shook Thomas' hand.

Thomas turned to leave and join his crew. This was their 12th mission. They were almost halfway through their runs. If they could make it to 30, they'd be sent home. He climbed on board and went to the radio room, placed the oxygen mask over his face and breathed deeply. It cleared his head somewhat and Thomas mentally thanked whoever had discovered this cure for those pilots who had imbibed a little too much before a mission.

The flight was uneventful. No fighters and a minimum of flak. At the base, he turned in his navigation log. Maybe the liquor helped, but in his opinion the log was the best he'd ever turned in to the debriefing officer. Then, he learned, they would fly again on the eighth.

11

Ten Minutes

On May 8, 1944, the B17 climbed and joined other bombers in the cloudy skies over England. It had been a smooth takeoff.

Thomas adjusted his navigator's seat in the plane's nose section and glanced out toward the clouds that quickly enveloped the ground beneath the plane. In one sense, he felt somewhat sheltered when the plane joined other planes 25,000 feet above the English Channel. He imagined that the layer of clouds hid the Flying Fortresses from the flak of enemy fire. However, he knew it was a false sense of security.

German fighters could be just ahead, waiting. They would approach from the east; flying out of the sun to attack Allied planes. It was the Germans' favorite mode of attack. By approaching from that angle, they hit at the weakest point of defense for the Fortresses.

If the clouds cleared away so Thomas could verify their position, the inevitable bursts from German artillery could find them. Another attack on Berlin, another tempting of fate, the 180-pound navigator thought.

Thomas Fitzgerald, the bombardier sat in the very front of the nose section checking his instruments for the bombing run. Thomas wondered what he was thinking. Does he regard the clouds as a blessing or a curse? he wondered. There was always a mixture of fear and anticipation among the crews. Fear that they might not make it back from the mission, but anticipation of what battles lay ahead. Thomas knew it had been especially true today because the Fortresses were attacking Berlin for the second day in a row.

Hours passed. As they flew over the Netherlands, a group of B24s to the right of the B17s' formation drifted toward them. The B24s forced the B17s to adjust their position and move more towards the outer perimeter of the squadron of bombers.

Thomas felt uneasy. There wasn't any reason he should. This had happened before on flights over Europe. Yet, he couldn't shake the feeling that this was a bad beginning for their mission.

"We're north of where we should be," Thomas told Fitz. Then, the cloud cover cleared and he spied Hanover below them. When he looked to the southeast, he saw Brunswick in the distance.

About 10 a.m., Thomas took a fix on the ground and entered their position in his log. As he looked up, he felt an explosion and found himself thrown backwards landing on top of the bomber's escape hatch. At the same time, he felt a quick stab of pain along his back and arms.

The pain quickly faded away. He heard the voices of Harold Niswonger, the pilot and Rod Steele, his copilot trying to assess damage to the plane and injuries to the crew.

Better put my chute on, Thomas told himself.

However, his right arm wasn't working the way it should. Somehow, he managed to get his chest chute on. Then he started crawling back toward the navigator's guns.

My arm's numb, he thought. It was then that Thomas felt a prickling sensation in his back. He couldn't understand it. There was no pain, but he felt something sticking to him. He looked and saw blood seeping from a wound in his chest.

"Fighters, 10 o'clock," someone called. Two more explosions followed.

"Number 3 engine's out," Niswonger said over the intercom.

"Can't make it back to the desk," Thomas said as he pulled himself to his knees. He was now halfway between the hatch and the navigator's desk and shakily stood up. He felt the plane buckling as Niswonger tried to maintain control.

He was getting closer to the navigator's desk despite the plane's erratic plunging and bucking. Then, he felt as if someone had knocked his breath out.

Machine gunfire. It must have hit him. But he wasn't bleeding. At least he didn't think he was bleeding. However, there was still that sticky feeling that he had noticed earlier, a feeling that he refused to associate with being wounded.

There must be German fighters attacking us, Thomas thought. He raised his left hand and touched his jacket, feeling his wife Marie's picture in his breast pocket.

Through the commotion around him, he could see the bombardier moving toward him.

"We're on fire," Fitz told him.

Fitzgerald had his parachute on and was adjusting it. The intercom came on and Thomas guessed what the pilot would say before he heard the words.

"Jump!" Niswonger ordered.

Thomas found his way back to the escape hatch, pulled it open, hesitated for a moment, then bailed out. He felt the satisfying lurch of the chute opening like an umbrella above him. Looking toward the plane, he expected to see Fitz right behind him. He wasn't. Then he saw two more chutes.

"Count the chutes," he reminded himself. That's what they train us to do. He started counting. As he began, there was an immense flash and the plane blew up. A few moments ago engines had been aflame. Now, all he could see was a ball of fire in the morning sky. Thomas turned his head away not wanting to watch the plane as it disintegrated.

Can't think of the plane now. Concentrate on reaching the ground safely, he thought as he turned his attention toward finding an open field to land on. His chute began drifting toward a river, and using his good left arm, he adjusted the chute so he would land on earth rather than water. As he landed, he checked his watch. 10:10 a.m. Ten minutes had passed since his last navigation fix.

Looking around he saw Albert Grick; a waist gunner from his plane had landed close to him. The gunner took off his own chute and rushed over to the navigator.

"You're covered with blood, Thomas," Grick said as he helped him out of his parachute. "Let's hope we get picked up by the military and not any farmers nearby."

Thomas knew what he meant. There was more of an opportunity to survive if soldiers rather than villagers found you. Within minutes he saw German soldiers driving a canvas-covered truck in the distance.

"Did they all get out?" Albert asked as he looked toward the sky then back to his navigator.

"I don't think so," Thomas said. He felt unsteady. His arm hung by his side, useless.

"Do you know where we are?" the gunner asked.

"I think we're close to Verden."

"Not that it matters. We'll soon be prisoners of war," Albert said as the truck bore down on them.

It was no use trying to escape. The field they'd landed in provided no cover. So, they waited for the German soldiers to pull up.

"*Nichts scheissen*," Albert called out as he raised his hands in surrender while Thomas raised his left arm. The other wouldn't move. Finally, he raised it by lifting it with his left hand.

Thomas noticed the German guards laughing and grinning as they motioned them toward the back of their truck.

Scheissen? Thomas thought. Albert said *scheissen*. No wonder the guards were laughing. He should have said—*schiessen*.

"Why are the guards laughing?" Albert asked Thomas as the two moved slowly toward the truck.

Thomas smiled, "It's what you said, Albert. You said '*scheissen*'."

"Well, I said—Don't shoot. Didn't I?"

"No, you said—Don't shit."

"Oh!" Albert smiled sheepishly. "Well, anyway. They didn't shoot."

"No, they didn't," Thomas agreed.

For the first time since being shot down, the two men grinned at each other. The mix-up in words by Grick provided some needed levity for their new position as prisoners of the Third Reich.

Albert helped Thomas climb into the truck. As he sat down, Thomas looked toward the front of the truck. He cringed. He could see the dead bodies of other airmen. The bodies were piled on top of each other in the inner portion of the truck.

"Those are your dead comrades," a German soldier said when he noticed Thomas looking toward the bodies. "Now you know what awaits you when you attack us."

"How did they die?" he asked.

"Bullets, pitchforks. What difference does it make?" the soldier asked. "You're lucky we reached you first."

The German was right. Too many stories had reached the bases about bombing crews bailing out, only to be killed by civilians when they landed. He didn't say another word. Roderick Steele was already sitting in the truck waiting for them

"How many made it, Rod?" Thomas asked after he sat down.

"I don't know. But I don't think Niswonger got out."

Thomas looked toward the field behind them. A truck was leisurely scouring the field to pick up more bodies. He looked at his arm. It ached. This was the first time he'd even had a chance to check it. His right sleeve was shredded and covered with blood. When he looked closer, he saw that the lower part of his right arm, just above the elbow, had been gashed as if a knife had cut out a portion of it.

12

Prisoner of War

Prisoner of war! The words seemed hollow, almost devoid of meaning. Thomas knew many men had been shot down and were listed as prisoners of the Germans. He never thought it would happen to him. He and the other aviators always imagined it happening to someone else.

Someone else would be shot down. Someone else would be taken to a prison camp. Looking behind him and seeing the bloodied bodies of fellow aircrews was something he thought he'd never see. All of the crews felt the same way. They always expected to make it back.

He thought back to the raid on Berlin. Yes, there had been flak. But he didn't expect to ever be blown out of the sky by it. It surrounded them during their attacks. It had always been like a dark cloud, hovering on the horizon.

The German fighters were a nagging fear for any bomber crew. Now a prison camp awaited him. That would be the eventual destination of the other prisoners and himself. He looked out the back of the truck as the Germans transported the survivors away from where they had landed after parachuting.

Standing there, after parachuting, that was his last moment of freedom. His last opportunity to be the attacker had been in the air, not on the ground, a prisoner of the Germans. When his plane was shot down, he had landed on land belonging to the enemy. He was a trespasser for several minutes, then a prisoner, no longer in charge of his own destiny. What would Marie say? Would she know? Yes, they'd tell her. But when?

He had always looked forward, not behind. That's how he had survived when he was young. That's what had enabled him to look beyond the death of his father and being placed in an orphanage for 10 years. He'd learned to adapt. He'd also learned that he should never allow himself to be placed on the sidelines. If he allowed others to place him there, he'd not control his own destiny.

Now he was on the sidelines, forced to step aside and let others win the battles in the sky. It was a difficult role to accept, but he would adapt. He always had.

His mind kept going back to the suddenness of the change in his life. At one instant, he was navigating the bomber to its assigned target. The next he was in free-fall as a silk parachute floated him down to his enemy's grasp.

Thomas remembered the minutes of calm just before the attack. Ten minutes. That was all it took to reduce the plane to a blazing inferno. Ten minutes had meant machine gun bullets ricocheting through the plane and a cannon shell bursting behind him. And, what of the others? What were they feeling? Were they as numb and aching from the machine gun bullets as he? The bullets had glanced off his chest. A cannon shell that had cut a portion of his arm away like it was a doctor's scalpel. Had they experienced that? Better not to think about it. Better to find out what had happened.

"Why did the plane blow up?" Thomas asked Rod Steele as he tried to divert his mind from questions about their future.

"I don't know," the copilot replied. "I was too busy getting out."

"I think I saw a German fighter hit the plane," Robert Morrison, another member of the crew said. "It was just after I jumped."

"I think I saw that too," said Fitzgerald. "I know that I saw a fighter bearing down on us. Didn't you see him, Thomas?"

"No, I was blown back in the nose. All I saw and felt were bullets," he said.

He turned his attention to the other members of his crew. Thomas saw where shrapnel had left a fine splattering of blood on the fronts of Rod's legs. He saw Fitzgerald bending over and testing an ankle. The bombardier's ankle looked swollen. None of the survivors seemed to have escaped without reminders of the battle that had raged about them.

"Thomas you're covered with blood," Albert said. He had observed this when they first landed on German soil. Now he repeated his earlier observation as if he or the others could somehow find a way to staunch the seeping of the blood. Finally, it seemed to stop of its own accord. His shirt and uniform had served as a makeshift bandage, clinging to the wounds to stop the flow.

Thomas could see it and feel it. Did someone once call this a red badge of courage? No, it wasn't. It was a badge of pain. There was a burning sensation that seemed to run up and down his back. He must have been hit with shrapnel like Rod. Thomas fingered the picture of Marie in his breast pocket to see if it was still there. He felt it. However, he didn't take it out to look at it.

The truck with its living and dead occupants left the field and entered a nearby road. If anyone had any thoughts of escaping Thomas could see how useless the attempt would have been. There were several trucks behind them—all bearing the marks of the German army. He assumed the trucks carried soldiers as well as prisoners. Anyone attempting to find out for sure would be an easy target for the soldiers.

We have to be heading toward Verden, Thomas thought, as they continued along the narrow highway. Every bump in the road sent a stab of pain through his arm and caused him to break into a sweat.

"How's the arm, Thomas?" Steele asked as he broke the silence.

"I don't know Rod. It hurts like the devil."

"Maybe when we get to where they're taking us they'll do something for you," Grick said.

Thomas nodded. He hoped so. The pain made him feel dizzy. He couldn't wait until they were out of the truck and standing on solid ground.

The truck stopped. Thomas saw several barracks and an artillery regiment's headquarters.

"Out! Out!" Someone yelled from outside the truck.

The prisoners slowly climbed down, lined up and waited. German soldiers stood on either side of them with their guns at the ready. When Thomas and the others emerged, a German officer came up to their guards and ordered the soldiers to escort the prisoners to cells in the barracks.

"Separate the enlisted men from the officers and place them in different cells," the officer ordered. "Then, search them."

Methodically the soldiers patted them down, searching for any hidden weapons. When they touched his arm, Thomas staggered backwards and was kept from falling by his own men. He gritted his teeth and waited.

"He's got something in his breast pocket, Otto," one of the guards said. Warily they approached him. It would have been useless to resist. Too many guns pointed in his direction. The man addressed as Otto reached inside Thomas' jacket and quickly drew out the leather wallet containing the picture of Marie.

"Karl, look at this." Otto held up the wallet. Karl and three or four of the soldiers came over and looked at the wallet. The soldiers moved closer. Each looked at the wallet, then Thomas, as if they couldn't believe their eyes.

Thomas stared at the wallet. He reached over and gingerly touched the leather case the German held. It wasn't smooth. The bullet had gone through the wallet next to his chest ripping the inner half. Then, it exited, away from his heart.

"Your girl?" the man addressed as Karl asked, as he looked at the black and white picture of Marie with the mark of the passing bullet visible on her picture.

"My wife."

Karl fingered the outside of the wallet as if he still couldn't believe a bullet had penetrated through the case and not killed the airman before him.

"God has watched over you, lieutenant," Karl slowly returned the picture. "Keep the wallet."

Thomas stared at the thin layer of leather holding the picture of his wife. Then, he acknowledged the man's words with a slow nod of thanks.

The other men were searched and herded into cells. Rod and Tom Fitzgerald were placed in the same cell as Thomas. After the German soldiers left, they came over and stared at the leather wallet and Marie's picture.

"If ever a man is lucky to be alive, you are," said Rod.

Thomas held the picture for several minutes then placed it back in his pocket next to his heart.

Several hours later, the German officer commanding the artillery unit came in to see the prisoners.

"Have you had anything to eat?" he asked.

"No, sir," the men said in unison.

"Where are you from?" he asked casually.

"You know we can't answer that, sir," Rod said.

"Yes, I know."

"Where did you learn to speak English so well?" Thomas asked.

"In Chicago, I visited there once," the commander said. He waited for a response but Thomas just nodded and retreated to a corner of the cell to sit down.

He was exhausted. He did not want to be reminded of Chicago and Marie, at least not now.

"I'll order some soup and bread be brought in," the commander said.

"Thank you commander," Rod said.

They stayed at the artillery barracks until nightfall. Then, soldiers came in and wakened those that had fallen asleep.

"You are going to a Luftwaffe base," they announced.

The men followed the guards out to another truck and climbed aboard. Thomas felt weak. When would they do something about his arm? He would ask at the air base when they arrived. Again they disembarked from the truck and were taken to holding cells.

"Can you get me a medic?" Thomas asked one of the guards. "My arm is bad."

An hour later a medic came by and looked at the arm. "We can't do anything for you here," he said. "All I can do is put sulfa on it and give you a couple of aspirins."

Well, better than nothing, Thomas thought.

"You and some of the others will be taken to a hospital in Hanover," the medic continued. "They can probably do something there."

13

Wounded in Action

Thomas learned that the hospital in Hanover was a former university building. He and the other wounded prisoners were taken to a floor at the very top of the building.

"If your friends bomb this building, you'll go first!" one of the guards called out before bolting the door behind them.

He looked around the room. Thomas counted eight prisoners. One aviator had half his leg blown away below the knee. Another had his face covered with bandages.

The rubber from his oxygen mask must have melted into his skin, Thomas thought as his eyes came to rest on the man's burned hands and scorched uniform. He doesn't even have openings in the bandages so he can see. Is he blind? he wondered.

He studied the dank surroundings of the chamber. It looked as if it was about 12 by 14 feet in area. There was little light. But he could see that the double-decker beds were narrow and placed against the perimeter of the room.

There's barely enough space to stretch out, Thomas thought. So, he opted to sit down in a corner of the room and rest his back against a wall. The wall was cool to his touch. It reminded him that spring had not given way to the warmth of summer. He turned his attention to the other wounded men in the room. Fitzgerald, the bombardier from his plane, had a sprained ankle and seemed to be the least seriously wounded. Steele was there with his wounded leg full of shrapnel. Other prisoners appeared to have broken bones from the way they had landed after parachuting.

A few like Steele and himself the evidence of bullet wounds. Every so often, the man who had lost part of his leg would moan. A tourniquet had been placed around the leg to prevent further bleeding.

Thomas looked up at the wooden beams of the ceiling. They reminded him of his attic home in Bensenville and the orphanage. He sat in the cell, feeling the pain throbbing up and down his arm. A faint light outside the bolted door cast an eerie glow in the cell. He could barely make out the other prisoners. He noticed Rod Steele was awake and got up and walked over to where the co-pilot sat.

"When are they going to do something about that man's leg?" Thomas asked Steele and nodded toward the prisoner whose leg appeared to have no more than a bone sticking out from the knee.

Steele grimaced. "When they feel like it, maybe."

"When they feel like it?" Thomas repeated. It had never occurred to him that doctors just might choose to do nothing. Steele had to be wrong. The doctors couldn't just let a prisoner with the wound that man had go untreated. He looked uneasily toward the wounded man and his bloodied leg. Silently he retreated to the wall that he had leaned against earlier and lowered himself to the floor and waited for whatever the hospital would do next.

The following morning the guards took Thomas down to the main hospital section to have the doctors look at his arm. He sat in a chair opposite them listening, they spoke among themselves and Thomas heard them suggest there was a possibility of an amputation. He understood enough of the German to interrupt them.

"No! I don't want it amputated," he said. His voice trembled as he tried to control his emotions and fears.

The doctors looked at him in surprise. "You understand German," one of them said.

"Yes," Thomas responded. "I understand you are considering amputating the arm. I'll take my chances on it healing."

No way, no way were they going to take the arm, he thought. He couldn't let them. He had to keep the arm. He looked from one doctor to the other, afraid of what they might decide.

This time the doctors withdrew to discuss the prognosis so he couldn't hear. When they returned, one of them removed the old bandage and began cleaning the wound.

"We will not amputate," the doctor said. "I will clean it and put sulfa on it to prevent infection. However, you must understand you are taking a chance with your life. The wound may become worse."

"I realize that," Thomas said. "But it's my arm and it's my life."

"So be it," the doctor said. He treated the wound and signaled the guards to take him back to his cell.

The next day a doctor and two soldiers came into the cell. The physician motioned the soldiers over to the aviator whose mangled leg stuck out from a blanket.

"Get him to surgery!" the doctor ordered.

Without another word, the soldiers picked the man up and carried him out of the room. Thomas looked at the remaining men in the room. No one spoke. The quiet seemed to engulf them. They waited. Then, several hours later the soldiers brought back the wounded man.

"They amputated his leg," Thomas whispered.

Steele nodded.

The other men looked away as if afraid to acknowledge what had occurred. It was obvious the man was in shock. He continued to moan, but he also seemed to be reaching down to try and feel for a leg no longer there.

As Thomas's wounds throbbed, and the arm became increasingly painful despite the Germans cleaning the wound and redressing it, he veered between thinking of the years before the war and his being a prisoner.

Thomas could feel himself perspiring and guessed he probably had a fever. Desperately he tried to shift his attention to the cell and its occupants. Rod was asleep. He could barely make out the shallow breathing of the copilot. The man whose leg had been amputated was still moaning and reaching for the leg that was no longer there.

The room was so dark that he could only see a few of his fellow prisoners. Then, he heard the sound.

"Pick! Pick! Pick!"

What was it? A mouse? A rat? Or, perhaps something else was scurrying around the cell.

It continued, "Pick! Pick! Pick!"

Some of the other prisoners stirred. Rod was now awake and looking toward him with a puzzled expression on his face. Light from the corridor filtered through the bars on their room. If he concentrated on the other men, he could see more of their features.

Thomas looked toward where the man with the bandages on his face sat. He suddenly realized—that's where the sound was coming from—the man was picking at his bandages. He's trying to find out whether he's blind, Thomas thought. He watched him with a mixture of dread and curiosity.

Would he be able to see?

He watched as the man shakily picked a hole through a thin layer of gauze covering his eyes. Finally, the man put his arms down and bent forward holding his head in his hands.

"I can see. I can see," the man gasped.

Thomas could hear him crying. He looked toward Steele and Fitzgerald who were also awake now. They all watched the man. Thomas was sickened at the sight of the scraped away bandages. However, he felt thankful that the prisoner wasn't condemned to a world of darkness. That would be hard to take for the rest of one's life.

It's bad enough just being in this darkened cell temporarily, Thomas thought. At least that man has some hope for the future. What will be the future for the amputee? he wondered.

Apparently, the thought crossed the mind of the other prisoners as well for their eyes strayed to the man on the floor. He was delirious. It sounded as if he was calling for someone.

Several guards entered the room.

"You prisoners well enough to travel will be removed to Frankfurt," a German lieutenant told them.

"What of this man?" Thomas asked as he pointed toward the amputee.

"His war is over," the lieutenant said. "He will be sent home."

The following day the guards arrived early and herded the men out to the corridor. The officer ordered them to line up just outside the heavy wooden door. "Come on, you are to leave immediately."

Thomas leaned against the wall. The prisoners then were pushed toward a stairwell and they climbed down the stairs to the street. Now, it seemed as if every step he took was an effort. As they gathered outside the door of the hospital, the men saw several German guards mounted on motorcycles. The prisoners were shepherded into the street and the guards lined up directly behind them.

"Where are we going?" Thomas asked one of the guards.

"To the rail station," the man answered. "Now move."

When Thomas and the others were brought to the hospital during the night, they had no opportunity to see the city. Now, as they marched through the city's center, they saw the bombed out remnants of buildings on either side. Just ahead on the right, he saw two burned up streetcars.

Why streetcars? Why these buildings? Were there any military targets near here? he wondered. Were any of the other prisoners wondering the same thing? As if in answer, Rod Steele shook his head. Steele looked around him and then stared straight ahead. There were a few civilians out and Thomas and the others could hear the muttering as they moved on. It was a short walk to the city's rail station. When they arrived, they boarded a train to Frankfurt.

On reaching Frankfurt, the men were placed in individual cells before interrogation. The cell Thomas found himself in was eight by ten feet. There was a single light hanging from the ceiling. After he entered the closet-like room, the guards turned off the light. The only light now available came from a small high window opposite the door.

Thomas stood only a moment. He had had little time to make out the outlines of the cell before the guards darkened the room. However, he didn't care. Feeling his way along the wall, he found an empty corner, lowered himself down to the floor and fell into an exhausted sleep.

The following morning Thomas was shaken awake by one of the German guards. The light was on in his cell and a German officer began asking him questions about his unit.

"You know I can only give you my name, rank and serial number," Thomas said.

The officer asked him a few more questions. When Thomas didn't reply, he turned and left.

A few hours later, the guard entered his cell again, "You are to come with me," he said.

Thomas struggled to his feet and followed the man to a room where the officer who had questioned him earlier waited. The officer sat there, looking at a sheaf of papers. Then, raising his eyes, he looked at his prisoner.

"Your name is Thomas Thomas," the officer said. "You are a navigator with the 96th Air Group out of Snetterton-Heath."

Thomas stared straight ahead. How did he know this? he wondered.

The interrogator seemed to realize what he was thinking. "We know much about your military, thanks to the superiority of our intelligence network," he said.

"I am only required to give my name, rank and serial number," Thomas responded as he had before when he was questioned. He was still stunned at how much the interrogator knew.

"Lieutenant, let's make this easy on you," the German said as he motioned him to a seat. "You are wounded. You are surprised at how much I know. If you will agree to sign this document stating who was in your crew, you can get treatment for your wound."

So, that's why they've done nothing further in treating my wound, Thomas thought. They can use that against me. And, he had the sinking feeling that they might continue to deny him treatment until he broke down. He vowed he would give them as little information as possible.

The officer walked over with the list and thrust it before him. Thomas read the names. Not one name on the list was a member of his crew. He looked up at the interrogator. He knows that they aren't from my crew, he realized. What is he doing? If I refuse, what will happen? I don't know anyone on that list. What do I have to lose?

Finally, Thomas agreed, "I'll sign the list," he said. The interrogator handed him a pen and Thomas signed where he indicated.

"Take him back to his cell," he ordered.

"What about treatment for my arm?" Thomas asked.

"What treatment?" the officer dismissed him.

Bastard, Thomas thought. He then turned on his heel and followed the guard back to his cell.

The following day the German guards took him out of the cell and moved him to a barracks that contained other prisoners awaiting transportation to a prisoner of war camp. Two more days followed. Then he, Steele and some of the others were moved to a depot in the center of Frankfurt.

Thomas stared at the bombed station. Steel that had served to strengthen the top of the building was gone. It lay open, like an engineering model, with chairs placed in its center. The room was exposed to the elements and all the windows were missing.

"We really hit that building," Thomas whispered to Steele.

Steele didn't even nod. He looked straight ahead at an incoming passenger train.

Thomas heard the mutterings on either side of them as the soldiers, with bayonets at the ready, escorted them to the rail side.

"Dirty Americans," one yelled. "You bomb women and children," another called out.

Other passengers raised their voices angrily.

And what have you done? Thomas thought. What of Poland, France and other countries you've invaded?

Best to show no emotion, no weakness. He tried to stand straight and the effort caused the sweat to break out on his face. He was taken to a compartment housing six prisoners, one of whom was a lieutenant colonel. Thomas sat down next to him and tried to get comfortable.

"Lieutenant," the colonel said. "You take the window and rest that arm against it," he ordered.

Thomas nodded his thanks and exchanged seats. Even the effort to get up and move, then brace his arm against the window seemed to be more than he could bear. He gritted his teeth as the train started to move. He'd never much noticed the swaying motion that a train had. Nor had he been aware of the bumps that were a part of every rail journey. Now, every bump, every change in motion seemed to register double what it actually was.

Thomas knew a week-and-a-half had passed since they were shot down. There had been no opportunity to let Marie even know he was alive. The train stopped and he and the others disembarked to trucks waiting near the tracks.

Again, he climbed into waiting transports like the ones that had picked him up after he parachuted from his bomber. German soldiers watched his every move. Even if he had wanted, there was no way he could escape. For now, he accepted his position. Then, the prison camp with its guard towers came into view.

"This is Stalag Luft III," an English-speaking soldier announced. And, he motioned the prisoners down from the truck.

14

Stalag Luft III

As Thomas and the others entered the prison camp, he was surprised at the number of men who stood watching them. The camp was huge. On the east, south and southwest were forests of pines. Pinecones were just beginning to form on the branches.

Thomas turned his attention toward the gate of the camp. He stared at the watchtowers that were strategically placed 70 meters apart along the barbed wire surrounding the compound. He could barely make out the men in German uniforms. They stood atop the towers. Each tower appeared to house a machine gun. He could see metal barrels thrust out into that May morning, reminding him that he was a prisoner and entering a new stage of his life.

When he became a part of a bomber's crew based in England, he knew the date of his arrival. On March 26, he flew his first mission out of Snetterton-Heath. The time of leaving on that flight to Europe was seared into his memory, just like the day in April when he heard that Knobby Walsh had been shot down. He'd known almost instinctively that Knobby was dead. But his being a prisoner now would make it possible to know for sure. The other prisoners would know his fate.

What day is it? he wondered. May 14 or May 16? He'd lost count. He waited for the signal to move into the camp enclosure and while he waited he scanned the faces of the prisoners in the compound. No Knobby. Was there anyone there he knew? Yes. He thought he saw some men he'd met in navigator training. They waved, acknowledging his presence, but no one spoke.

How could there be so many prisoners of war? he wondered. Still, there'd been hundreds and hundreds of planes. And, many of his friends had been shot down—killed, missing in action or prisoners. Few returned once their planes were hit. He thought again about Knobby. Was he here? He didn't see him. His eyes took in the men near the gate. They seemed thin. Their uniforms were worn. Their faces strained. Yet, they didn't appear at all disheartened.

When he caught the expression in their eyes, he detected resilience as if being a prisoner meant just waiting for the time when they were no longer prisoners but victors in the war. He had the feeling that these men expected to emerge soon from the boundaries encircling them in the camp. As he studied his fellow prisoners, he realized that they like him were survivors. They had been shot down, or taken prisoners in some battle he may have never seen.

He'd seen one or two men he knew. However, the silence bothered him. The Sagan prisoners said nothing to him, or Rod, or any of the other prisoners. Upon entering the compound, Thomas saw a second parallel fence of barbed wire next to the other fence. Ten feet from the fence he saw another low wooden fence about a foot high. That fence formed an inner line close to the wire.

In the space between the fences was more wire, coiled and tangled. Just beyond the fences, he saw another area, which appeared to house a similar compound to the one he was entering. How many compounds made up the prisoner of war camp? It seemed to cover acres. The last time he'd seen acreage like this it had been when he was an orphan at Bensenville, where acre upon acre had been used to raise crops. Here, with the forests in the distance, he decided it was unlikely it had ever been used for food, pasture maybe, but not to raise farm crops.

Thomas and the other prisoners were escorted deeper into the compound. Now that he was inside, he could get a better estimate of the number of prisoners in the compound. At first, he had thought there were only a hundred or a hundred-and-fifty men in Stalag Luft III. He quickly revised this estimate. There must be close to 300 men in the one compound. He, Rod and the bombardier were assigned to the same wooden barracks, Block 160. The Block housed several rooms. Each room housed 12 men. He was assigned to a room 12 by 10 feet housing three triple deck beds, a table in the middle and a small stove.

Block 160 was close to a campfire pool and a cookhouse. To the north was a gate separating the prisons from guardroom and coal shed. Beyond the coal shed was another gate leading to the German guards' quarters. He paid scant attention to that portion of the camp. All he wanted to do was get into his new quarters and lie down. After entering the barracks, Thomas sunk into a lower berth exhausted. His arm was useless. He wouldn't have been able to climb to a higher bunk if he wanted. Still, no one spoke to the new prisoners. What were they waiting for? After a few minutes, a prisoner appeared before the new arrivals.

"Each of you will need to be questioned by our officers," the man said.

"Why?" Thomas asked.

"You have to be cleared before we tell you about the camp."

Thomas slowly stood up. He thought he could at least rest before meeting the other prisoners.

"Why don't you take this man first?" Rod Steele said as he motioned toward Thomas. "He's been shot up and is pretty exhausted."

The prisoner nodded. "Follow me," he ordered.

Thomas fell in behind him. He walked across the compound and entered a room being used as an office. Inside the room were several officers. They introduced themselves as Operations Col. W. W. Airing, Chief of Staff Colonel Jack Jenkins and Lt. Col. Darling, in charge of personnel.

"When were you shot down?" Airing asked.

"How long were you in solitary?" Darling questioned him and carefully took down his responses.

"What did you tell them?" Colonel Jenkins continued.

Thomas mentioned the list of men that was supposed to be members of his crew.

"That's a common technique," Airing said. "You didn't tell them anything else?"

"No, but they seemed to know where I flew out of and what group I was with."

Airing didn't seem surprised.

"You've been identified by a couple of men already here," said Lt. Col. Darling. "We'll brief you in a few days on procedures."

"How many prisoners are here?" Thomas asked.

"You mean in all of Stalag Luft III?"

"Yes." "There's close to 6,000 men."

Thomas gasped. "That many?"

Yes. The camp covers about 25 acres. The compound you are in is called West Compound. There is an East Compound occupied by British prisoners. There is also a Center Compound, a North Compound, a South Compound and Balaria, which is north of Sagan. The German troops occupy the center of the five compounds. Sagan is about 100 miles southeast of Berlin in lower Silesia. The entire area used to be part of a forest. You probably saw remnants of that forest on your arrival. Most of the forest area was cleared and a prisoner-of-war camp was constructed."

"All attempts at escape must be approved by the officers of the camp," Darling said. "We don't want you to make an attempt without knowing the terrain, the language, or have the necessary papers." He winked and Thomas smiled. He knew exactly what the colonel meant.

"Do you speak German?" Airing asked.

"Fairly well, Sir."

"Good. You may be able to train those who don't."

"Security is tight here," Colonel Jenkins informed him. "You may have heard that there was an escape last March from the British sector. It came to be called 'the Great Escape.' Most were recaptured and many were executed. Since then, there have been constant checks by the guards."

"You saw the low wooden fence as you entered the compound?" Airing asked.

"Yes," Thomas answered.

"Do not go into the area between the low fence and the outer fence," Airing continued. "The Germans usually warn you, but if you do not respond, they will open fire. They will kill you. Do you understand?"

"Yes, sir."

"Good. Now return to your barracks. Your barracks captain will tell you what else you need to know."

Darling motioned toward Thomas' arm. "Have you been given any treatment for that arm?"

"Not much, sir. They cleaned it and put sulfa on it."

We do have a medical officer," Airing said. "He doesn't have much equipment but don't hesitate to seek him out."

Thomas nodded. He hoped it wouldn't be necessary. He saluted as best he could and started to turn away.

Colonel Jenkins stopped him. "Oh by the way Thomas, we are called *Kriegies*. If you haven't heard the term before, it is short for *Kriegsgefangen*. Most prisoners don't understand German. However, you already know it means prisoner of war."

"I understand its meaning sir," Thomas said. He turned and the *Kriegie* that had escorted him to the leaders of the camp took him back to his barracks.

A week passed. Thomas could do little and his arm continued to bother him. He noticed that red streaks were beginning to spread downward from the upper arm. Could this be the forerunner of gangrene? Each day they seemed to be getting worse. The other prisoners in the room seemed to be avoiding him too.

Rod Steele approached him. "Thomas, there's something wrong with your arm. You're beginning to smell. Get to a doctor."

That same day Thomas reported to the makeshift hospital for prisoners. The first person to greet him was a doctor who had been captured in North Africa, Dr. Barks. He took one look at his arm and told him he'd be staying at the hospital for several days.

"I've got to get that infection down," Barks said. "If I don't, you could lose the arm."

The doctor prepared a hot compress and put it on the wound and Thomas settled in as a patient in Stalag Luft III. Every few hours the doctor changed the compress and removed the outer scab of the wound.

"It has to heal from the inside out," he explained. "Not only will we need to take care of the infection but the bullet probably broke a bone in your arm. After the infection is cleared, we'll provide you with a cast so the bone will heal."

"I see."

"Thomas, I also looked at your back. It looks as if the cannon shell that exploded behind you in the front of the plane shattered and some of the metal ended up in your back. I'm guessing, but I think it probably also burrowed into the back of your head. This means, over time, some of it may work itself to the surface of the skin. I don't know how much metal entered there, but it does look pretty pockmarked. I can't do anything about that. I'm not sure even a surgeon back in the States could help you there."

"Then it's just something I have to live with?"

"I'm afraid so." During the days that followed, Thomas heard a loudspeaker and listened as it gave news in German to the *Kriegies*.

The doctor listened and then said, "The Jerries have their version of the news of the war. We have ours. Somewhere, in between, is the truth."

Thomas laughed.

"And, what's the general consensus? Are we winning the war?"

"Yes, we're winning. However, we'll continue to lose men, good men."

"Any word on the invasion?

"No, but I and the other men feel it will happen very soon. After all, this is nearly the end of May. We pretty much have control of the skies. I don't think the Germans can defeat us. Don't forget we also have the Russians keeping them busy to the east."

About a week after their conversation, the doctor allowed Thomas to return to his barracks. The infection was gone. Now all Thomas had to do was wait for the wounds to heal. And he had to write Marie. Let her know he was okay. He wouldn't mention being wounded. That would only cause her concern.

He returned to his barracks, but a few weeks later he was back at the hospital. It felt like he had boils on the back of his neck.

"The pain's become more intense each day, Doc," Thomas explained as he sat down in a chair while Dr. Barks examined his neck. Every touch of the doctor's hand caused Thomas to wince in pain. Finally the doctor stopped the examination.

"What you've got is a carbuncle, Thomas," he explained. "It's caused by the metal that entered your back before you bailed out. It's like a boil in that it grows inward. However, it's more dangerous than a boil. We'll have to do something about it."

"What do you mean?" Thomas asked.

"You've got not one but two carbuncles and they'll have to be lanced. I'll have to cut them out."

Thomas watched as he motioned to two prisoners working in the hospital. Then the doctor took a sharp knife and poured iodine on it.

"We have no anesthetic, Thomas. These men will have to hold you down while I lance the carbuncles and dig out the stems that are growing inward."

Reluctantly Thomas sat in the chair while the prisoners moved into position on either side of him. One grasped his good arm and shoulder. The other man held onto his other shoulder and cast. At the same time, they pressed down on him, holding him in position. He felt the knife go in and a wet substance began to run down his neck.

"Puss," he thought. Then the knife dug deeper and Thomas clenched his teeth. The pain came in waves. The waves were like fire, burning as they engulfed him. He broke into a sweat. As he did so, he could feel the other prisoners placing more weight on his arms in an effort to hold him still.

"Get it over," he muttered. "Get it over." The blade cut deeper and Thomas thought he'd pass out from the pain. After what seemed hours, but was probably only a half-hour, the prisoners released him.

"Okay, Thomas. We're done," Barks said. "Stay where you are and I'll put some antiseptic on it and bandage you up."

"I couldn't get up now if I wanted to, Doc," Thomas said. He waited as the sting of the antiseptic hit the raw wound where the doctor had cut into the carbuncles. And, gasped at the pain. "Will I have to go through this again," Thomas whispered.

"I hope not. But that metal is a permanent part of you now. It may just work its way out in time."

Thomas wondered if he could make it back to the barracks.

"You're pretty weak, Thomas. I'd stay the night if I were you."

"I don't want to make this a regular habit, Doc. But, this time I think I'll take you up on that offer."

15

Life as a Prisoner

During the time that Thomas was healing from his wounds, he felt like an outsider looking in on the efforts of his fellow prisoners. He could not help with the chores in the barracks except in drying dishes and even that was awkward with one hand because his arm remained in a sling while it slowly healed. Yet, he was beginning to know the others in camp, through coaching the baseball team, playing chess, and taking classes or simply walking around the perimeter of the camp.

Thomas noticed there were very few wounded Air Force prisoners in the camp. He soon learned the reason. A pilot or crew that was shot down usually walked away from the experience unscathed, or they were dead. There was seldom a midway point. This had been the fate of his friend Knobby Walsh. Others in his crew survived. Knobby hadn't. Yet, Thomas had been the exception to this fact, as had a few others in the camp. Why was he one of the lucky ones? He didn't know. He touched the picture of Marie, remembering how the Germans had looked at it and how his own crew had reacted. His life must have been spared for a reason. He found himself thinking more in terms of God's will than he had ever before. His life meant something as long as he never gave up and faced the future day by day. The future he saw in this war favored the Allies, no matter how much the Nazis tried to convince the *Kriegies* otherwise.

He listened as the Germans broadcast their own version of the war each day, while awaiting the broadcasts from the Allies at night. Somewhere in between the Germans' version and the Allies' version was the truth about the progress of the war. Since he could do little to assist the men in his barracks, Thomas carried a tube for the prisoner's radio during the day. In the evening, the tube was put together with other parts of the radio so they could get news from the BBC during the evening. The prisoners usually moved the radio around so the Germans couldn't locate and destroy it.

Thomas and the others knew a landing on the coast of Europe was close at hand. He had been aware of the preparations in England. When the invasion

106

finally came in early June, he could see the uplifting effect it had on his fellow *Kriegies*. He could also see the manner in which the Germans reacted. The guards were older now. Some were even veterans of World War I. These older guards took the place of the younger Germans sent to the front to fight the Russians or to defeat the Allies in France or Italy.

"They must know that they are defeated," Thomas told Steele one day as they walked around the camp's perimeter. "Oh, they know," Rod agreed. "But until their higher command surrenders they have little choice but to continue the war."

The Germans checked the barracks twice a day. They were determined to guard against a repeat of the earlier escape that had raised the ire of Hitler to such an extent that he had many of the prisoners executed who took part. The escape not only resulted in the killing of some of the British prisoners, it also resulted in the court martial and execution of the German commander of the prison camp, Col. Von Lindeiner. For a time, the Luftwaffe lost control of the camp to the SS. The command of the camp was returned to the Luftwaffe after Hitler was informed good treatment of the prisoners was necessary to ensure the continued good treatment of German prisoners of war.

Despite their having experienced a mass escape by the *Kriegies*, the guards seldom discovered the tunnels that honeycombed the prison. The first few nights in Barrack 160, Thomas heard a sound underneath the floors of the barrack. He looked toward one of the prisoners who had been at the prison longer than him and asked about the noise.

"It's the ferrets," the man explained.

"Ferrets?"

"Yes, we call the Germans who search under the barracks ferrets."

"Ferrets is a good name for them," Thomas acknowledged with a grin. He watched as one of the men 'accidentally' spilled dishwater and let it drip down between the cracks of the floor. Then, he heard some expletives that reminded him of the time one of the boys at the Home had hit the chicken man with the pellets from the BB gun.

Bensenville was a long way away from Germany, a very long way, he thought. And, Marie seemed even further away. He hadn't written her yet. He must do that. She must be searching frantically for information about him.

Meals at Stalag Luft III were sparse. When he first arrived at the camp, the food parcels provided by the American Red Cross to supplement the food at the camp were meant to sustain an average person one week. However, instead of a full parcel, the Germans only gave the prisoners half a parcel per person. That half parcel usually consisted of a chocolate bar, raisins, prunes, crackers, cigarettes, powdered milk and Spam. Thomas didn't smoke. So he traded his ration of cigarettes to the other men in the camp or to the guards for other items—paper for writing, food, anything to make his days and nights more bearable.

The full parcel that the Red Cross provided one prisoner each week was supposed to consist of:

powdered milk	- 1 can	biscuits	- 1 can
spam	- 1 can	coffee	- 4 oz.
corned beef	- 1 can	jam or orange preserves	- 1 can
liver paste	- 1 can	prunes or raisins	- 1 can
salmon	- 1 can	sugar	- 8 oz.
Cheese	- 1 can	chocolate	- 4 oz.
Margarine	- 1 can	soap	- 2 bars
cigarettes	- 5 packages		

However, the reality was quite different and the men felt the difference.

The Germans provided the prisoners with a weekly staple equal to one pound per man. It included bread, sugar, cheese and potatoes. When they provided sausage, it usually consisted of bloodwurst (which most prisoners could not eat) and a small summer sausage. The vegetables provided might include kohlrabi, cabbage, or turnips. Split pea soup was served almost every day. The Germans also gave them a slice of bread and ersatz jam, a vegetable concoction that substituted for jam or butter.

The prisoners never had enough to eat. Thomas soon learned to quell the hunger that was a daily companion by drinking water whenever he felt hungry. As he and the others struggled to keep up their courage and survive, he found himself literally shrinking in size. He had entered the camp weighing almost 190 pounds. By July, his weight had dropped to 165 pounds. One of the prisoners in his barracks figured that they were eating 667 calories a day.

Thomas would lie on his bed and dream of the food he was missing. The dreams were painful reminders of the daily routine. The prisoners did manage to keep the barracks clean and the American officers would inspect the camp to make sure the rooms housing the prisoners didn't become a haven for pestilence which might attack them in their weakened condition.

Every day he joined the men in front of his barracks for roll call in the early morning and at about 1700 hours at night. Neither rain nor heat kept the German commander from performing this rite of inspection. After a slim meal in the morning, usually hickory nut coffee, bread and ersatz jam, Thomas helped clean up before beginning a walk around the perimeter of the camp. He tried to walk around the perimeter of the camp 12 to 14 times a day. Yet, with each step, he didn't feel stronger or more energized. Instead, he felt weaker. Soon, he would sit down with three or four other prisoners and while away the time by digging at the several stumps littering the site where the prison camp stood. Each man would take a spoon and begin to dig at the stump. A spoonful at a time, they removed the dirt from around the roots of the tree.

"It takes time, but what else do we have to do?" one prisoner said. Thomas agreed. "I'd like to take part in some of the sports," he said. "But until this arm gets better, I can't." "You can always manage one of the teams or take some of the classes," a fellow digger said. "Take a look at those playing. They don't have the energy to play long," he added as he bent forward to scoop up some more dirt. Thomas studied the men. They were too weak to play a whole game of ball. The half-rations they received were robbing them of energy. Fortunately, there was no sickness in the camp. If this continued, they wouldn't have any defense against dysentery or other diseases that might invade the camp. The one thing that might prevent it, even with the loss of weight, was the cleanliness the American officers insisted upon as a means of keeping the prisoners somewhat healthy.

However, one of the prisoners in the barracks was beginning to cause a real problem. He had been captured shortly after Thomas and he objected to washing in the cold water, which was the only way the *Kriegies* had to keep clean. It wasn't too noticeable in the beginning, but after a while there was a distinct stink coming from his end of the barracks room. Thomas and a few of his fellow prisoners decided to take the matter up with Commander John Dunn, who was in charge of the barracks.

"This guy is really bad," Thomas told the commander. "We don't even want to be in the same room with him."

"That's right, Commander." Rod Steele wrinkled his nose in disgust. "If it was up to me I'd throw him out of our barracks entirely. No one wants to be near him."

"Have you talked to him?" Dunn asked.

"Yes, he won't listen," another man said. "And, I'm bettin' you've noticed him too."

"We have," Dunn said. "I think the whole barracks has."

"Well, what can we do?" Thomas asked. "When I was at the Home in Bensenville there was a kid who brought Limburger cheese to school. He smells worse than that."

"Certainly isn't my normal military problem to solve," Dunn admitted with a laugh.

He quickly sobered up when he saw the frowns his comment aroused.

"Come on, Commander. We can't take this any more," a thin bespectacled *Kriegie* said.

"Let's see," Dunn paused. "This calls for the highest level of military consideration," he said and burst out laughing. "I'm sorry men. I know it can't be pleasant. Hell, we're down the hall and we smell him too. Does he go outside?"

"Yeah, why?" Thomas asked.

"Well, what about the fire pool."

"The fire pool," Thomas repeated. "I think I know what you're thinking."

"Yeah, grab him and throw him in," Dunn said. "But you'll have to do it when he wanders over there."

"Agreed," said Rod. They returned to their area. The following day Thomas carried a bar of soap in his sling waiting for the moment of attack, while Rod and the others watched the man's every move.

"He's moving towards the fire pool," Thomas whispered to Rod. He glanced around the camp and noticed the other prisoners seemed to be watching them. There was a strange silence, a silence of anticipation.

"Operation Skinny Dip is about to get under way," Rod said. From various quarters six of the men gathered near the prisoner whose every move seemed to unleash an aura of stench. The target moved closer to the fire pool. As he did so, he seemed oblivious his fellow *Kriegies* were close behind him. Then, he glanced behind him, noticing the men who were nearly upon him. Directly in front of him was the pool. He looked at the pool and his fellow prisoners. A look of comprehension crossed his face, as if he knew what was to come.

"No!" he screamed as he tried to flee. It was too late. The hunters were upon their prey in a moment. There was a concerted rush. The black-haired prisoner struggled. But, it was six against one.

"Grab him," someone yelled. "Even holding a leg is like holding a stinking, rotting log," another complained as he tried to hold the offending appendage at arm's length. "Now, together, lift," Rod called as he hung on desperately to the wriggling prisoner. For a moment, the offensive prisoner was held suspended above the fire pool. Then, the *Kriegies* threw him into the cold water. He fell in back first, showering those around him.

"I didn't want a bath too," sputtered one of the men. Water dripped from his face and shirt. Another tried to keep his footing in the area around the pool area, which had suddenly been coated with puddles of water. Struggling to his feet in the middle of the pool, the prisoner tried to climb out one end, then another. Each time he was pushed back into the water. In retaliation, he splashed water on those who guarded the walls of the fire pool. The pool was now beginning to take on a definite brown cast. Prisoners from other barracks began to gather around it. Thomas removed the bar of soap from his sling and threw it at the man in the pool.

"Wash yourself," he said.

"And, don't come out until you're done," the men yelled as they continued to stand around the pool to fend off any further attempts at escape. After several attempts to get out of the fire pool, the offending prisoner gave in and slowly removed his clothes. He hung them on the side of the pool and began to clean himself. The men waited, not willing to leave until the object of the attack had succumbed to their demands. Then, the men began laughing and pointing at the helpless prisoner. The prisoner tried to make a break for it but was quickly pushed back into the cold water. All of the men surrounding the fire pool were soaked. Now they were not only laughing at the man in the center of the pool but at their own bedraggled appearance.

"I've washed myself,' the prisoner pleaded. "Let me out. I'm freezing."

"Wash your clothes too," Rod ordered and threw them at the man. Sullenly the man complied, all the while keeping an eye out for an opportunity to escape. And he again draped the clothes on the firewall. Finally, the men relented and allowed him out of the pool. He stood there, soaked and naked from head to ankles. During his time in the water, he had kept his shoes on and they squeaked as he attempted to take a step away from the fire pool. Again, the men burst out laughing. One of them, between guffaws, threw the clothes that had been draped over the fire pool at the retreating prisoner. Then, turned away and almost collapsed with laughter in the arms of a buddy.

Operation Skinny Dip was a success. "If you don't continue to keep yourself clean, we'll throw you in again," one of the men told him. The man scurried away, dressing as he left. The look of fear in his eyes was acknowledgement enough that they would never have to throw him in the pool again. Thomas looked at Rod. He was as soaked as he was. They staggered away from the pool, laughing so hard that tears rolled down their cheeks. "I'll never forget this," Thomas said as he looked at their roommate's bare behind fleeing into the barracks. "Nor I," said Rod.

In the days following the forced cleaning of the prisoner in the fire pool, Thomas returned to the routine of digging out the stumps that surrounded the barracks. He would sit down with other prisoners, spoon in hand, and work at digging up the remnants of the trees that had been cut down when the Germans cleared the land for the prison camp. He sat, day-by-day, digging down underneath the cut-off trunk to get to its taproot. Then, he and the other prisoners borrowed an axe from a prison guard and chopped out the remainder of the stump. What wood they cut up they took back and used with the coal briquettes to help keep themselves warm when the temperature dropped at night. Or, they used the wood and coal to heat a meal at night from the sparse Red Cross packet given them by the Guards.

Thomas tried to keep active. He was itching to get involved in some kind of sports. So, he began managing the barracks softball team. When he wasn't managing the team, he began reading some of the books donated to the camp by the YMCA. The "Y" also made another contribution. They sent sporting equipment to the men. In addition, an item that they forwarded in the middle of summer was ice skates, which could be clamped on the bottom of a shoe for skating. The men took one look at the skates and quickly adapted them for another use—wire cutters. When the guards inspected the barracks, they found the would-be skates adapted and shaped into escape gear and confiscated the skates.

Each week the *Kriegies* went to the prison gate to greet new prisoners who were brought to the growing prison. Besides the newly captured prisoners, slave laborers also visited the camp. They came once a week to clear out ashes dumped in a central storage facility. However, it wasn't just ashes that were disposed of at the site. Prisoners dumped a mixture of ashes and soil from the tunnels they dug beneath the camp for the laborers to cart away from the camp. The soil was heavier than the ashes and Thomas often wondered if the Germans would ever check out what the laborers were removing. They didn't. The laborers themselves would wink and carry out the soil. It seemed as if they were happy to take part in at least some effort to escape.

To the Germans, these men were slave laborers. To the prisoners, they were comrades, united in their dislike of the Nazis. Not one of them ever betrayed the POWs to the Germans. He was certain of this. For no guard questioned the prisoners about the mixture of soil and ashes left for the laborers. Thomas knew the laborers must face worse treatment than the prisoners of war under the control of the Luftwaffe. They were dressed in rags and looked as if they were starving. Still, they went about their tasks at the camp without a word. Seeing them, Thomas wondered if the stories he had heard about the treatment of the Jews in Europe were true.

He managed to write a brief note to Marie in late June. It took time to write the note because he had to hold his wrist with his good arm and move the hand holding the pen to write. He did not mention his difficulty in writing. Instead, he assured her he was okay. And he received a note from her in response to his letter. He was allowed to send notes out twice a month. But he could receive letters and he learned he could also request items of clothing or food from home. While walking across the camp one day, Thomas and several of the men heard a roar overhead. "It's coming from *Landshut*," Thomas said. "I think it's some kind of plane but can't make it out."

"You're right, Thomas," Commander Dunn said. "It is coming from *Landshut*. As I understand it the Germans test planes there." "What kind?" "They call them jets. If they're as fast as they seem, we're going to have problems with them." Thomas continued to look at the streak of white following the mysterious object.

"Jets?" he repeated. "That's what some say." "Well, maybe they don't have many of them if they're experimental." Dunn nodded.

Thomas looked at the sky one more time. Then, he left the barracks commander and walked toward the perimeter of the camp. He had to keep up his routine of walking. He fell in with another prisoner and they talked about the Allied landing off the coast of France. The Allies had a foothold. Each day, they discussed the same topic. How much longer would they be prisoners of war?

In late July, the loud speaker-system of the Germans made a brief announcement about foiling a plot against der Fuhrer. The prisoners gathered in small groups talking.

"The war must be going worse for them than we expected," Rod Steele announced.

"I think you're right," Thomas said.

"I'd like to find out exactly what happened. And, who took part in this attempt," Fitz said.

"Will the guards tell us?" Rod wondered.

"They may be too scared," Thomas said as he looked at some of the guards who were keeping their distance from the prisoners.

Later, they learned what had been broadcast on the BBC, but the explanation of the assassination attempt was minimal. Finally, word was passed to the barracks' officers from Col. Alkire. They, in turn, reported what the prisoners knew about the attempt.

"I'm passing on what Alkire has learned," the barracks captain informed them. "It seems as if there was an assassination attempt against Hitler. Some of the General Staff were rumored to be involved."

"Do we know who?" Thomas asked.

"I think the Nazis are still piecing that together." He continued, "But Alkire believes that some suspicions point to General Rommel."

"Rommel?" The men gasped in unison.

"What type of an attempt?" Thomas asked.

"Evidently a bomb exploded during a planning session where Hitler was present. He wasn't killed. Too bad. Some were. The man who planted the bomb has been executed. Others who apparently took part in the attempt were also executed. Hitler and the Nazis are scouring the German officer corps for anyone who might have been a part of the attack. I doubt we'll learn much more than that. The guards are afraid any mention of the attack could link them to the assassination attempt."

Several minutes of silence greeted this news. Finally, Rod Steele asked, "Any other news?"

"Yes. The Allies have broken out from the beachheads in France and are making good progress. They are probably a third of the way across France." This news brought a cheer from the men.

16

Cost of Freedom

In early June, Thomas went back to the hospital to have his arm checked. While he was there, Doctor Barks, motioned him toward the rear of the hospital.

"Take a look out the back window, Thomas," he said. Thomas walked over and stood with two of the hospital volunteers, watching what looked like a military ceremony in the distance. It was hard to determine exactly what was happening. He could see British officers with German guards. He noticed some urns close to them.

"The Brits are going to bury those urns, Thomas," Barks said. "You heard about the escape that occurred this past March?"

"Yes," Thomas replied.

"There was supposed to be about 200 taking part."

"Well, those are the remains of those in charge. The SS murdered 50 of the men they recaptured."

"But they were prisoners of war."

"Yes. However, they weren't in uniform. That was enough of an excuse, plus it was an embarrassment to Hitler. He wanted to set an example."

"I see," Thomas couldn't take his eyes off the urns that contained the ashes of the men who had tried to escape. "Is that what awaits anyone that makes a break for freedom?" he said.

"Maybe," Barks said. He began to look at Thomas's arm. "Your arm's doing well. But I think you should keep it in a sling. Come back in a week," he concluded as he finished the examination.

Thomas watched silently as a hole was dug in the sandy soil and one by one the urns disappeared into the opening. Then, the British officers covered the excavation with dirt and began placing rocks and stones on top of it, constructing a makeshift memorial. He continued to watch as the British officers stood at attention. They saluted and left the area accompanied by the guards. Rocks and stones marked the grave of the men who had planned the escape a few short months ago.

If the time came, Thomas knew he would also attempt to escape. He must. It was expected of those who were held prisoners. Still, the thought of attempting to break out of Sagan when the Allies were moving closer every day, made him wonder about the wisdom of making such an attempt. He knew that the camp officers were in the process of discussing escape efforts. Perhaps there would be a moratorium on attempts because of the constantly changing fronts of the Russians and the Allies.

In the meantime, the prisoners continued to dig tunnels. They masked their activities by mixing the dirt removed from the tunnels with the gardens that the *Kriegies* tended, or mixed it with the ashes the slave laborers carried out. Even the volleyball games, which took place each day, were a means to hide the tunnel soil. Prisoners walked onto the volleyball court, drew the strings of trousers that had a hidden compartment containing dirt from the tunnels and the players taking part in the games promptly mixed the emptied dirt into the soil.

Some of the men began to wonder how much longer this would continue. The barracks captain, Dunn, called a meeting to address the situation near the end of June.

"The Allies are making great progress," Commander Dunn said. "I know you all are wondering if we should continue to dig tunnels or wait to be freed."

"The problem now is more acute," Dunn continued. "If an escape attempt is made at the present time, there is a very real possibility that anyone caught making the attempt would be killed. You would be treated as spies and executed."

"Just like the Brits?" Thomas asked."

"Yes, just like the Brits," Dunn answered.

Silence greeted this statement. All of the men were aware of the fate of the leaders of the March escape attempt.

"Make the best of the situation until we're freed," Dunn said. "That means a moratorium on escape attempts for now. The members of the escape committee are in full agreement on this."

"But we're slowly starving," one of the prisoners objected. "We can't just give into the situation."

"I know," Dunn said. "But what choice do we have? If we wait, perhaps more of us will survive. Until we hear differently, we must wait out events. The committee thinks we might all be free by Christmas."

"That's good news," Thomas told Rod. "However, that other guy had a point. Do we want to take the chance of succumbing to starvation, while waiting for liberation?"

"I know, Thomas," Rod said. "We've all heard stories about the concentration camps holding the Jews. But we've got no proof they exist."

"And, if they do exist?"

"I don't know."

Thomas decided he'd concentrate on surviving on what he had. That day he wrote another letter to Marie, urging her to send as much food as possible when she wrote him. But, her letters were few. Why didn't he hear from her more often? When he mentioned this to the other prisoners, one said that he thought the Germans were interfering with the mail.

"Some of the men are asking their families to number the letters so they can keep track of what we receive and don't receive."

Thomas sat down on his bunk. He could only write one letter a month and he wanted to think about what to put in his next letter. In other corners of the room, he watched as some of the men meticulously wrote their letters home. He knew that here and there were men who had been selected by the allies to correspond not only with their families but to keep the Office of Strategic Services informed of pertinent military information from the camps. Within those letters was a coding, earmarking certain letters in their words with a meaning code decipherers would find before the letters reached their final destination.

However, Thomas was not chosen, nor was he trained for this task. Instead, his letters would be for Marie. Censors might read his handwritten correspondence. Yet, he was confident the majority of his letters would reach her intact.

◆   ◆   ◆

As the summer crept on Thomas played chess, attended shows the prisoners put together, read and walked the perimeter of the camp. He also began taking classes. He brushed up on his German. He read every book available in the limited library. The days dragged on. July came and went. Near the end of August, the *Kriegies* received some startling news. A general in the Allied command had been shot down. He would be joining the men and become senior officer of the compound.

"His name's Vannaman," Rod said.

"Not General Arthur V. Vannaman?" Thomas asked. "Why would a general from the 8th Air Force be here?"

"Maybe he's coming to prepare us for being liberated," one of the prisoners said.

"He'd risk being shot down just to tell us the Allies are coming? No way," another prisoner said.

"But why did he expose himself to capture?" a third prisoner asked.

"I heard he bugged Doolittle to let him fly," another responded. "He was actually shot down in June and the Germans wanted to send him to a special area for high officer prisoners."

"Yeah, I heard that too," Thomas said. "When captured, he insisted on being imprisoned with the rest of us. That speaks well of him."

"It speaks well of him, or he's a damn fool," another said. "Who'd want to insist on coming here?"

This remark brought a laugh from the men. They stood by the gate watching as the general was brought through the entrance. He seemed in good physical shape.

"Don't see any wounds," Rod said.

"No, I don't either," Thomas said. "But I heard he was injured and spent four weeks in the hospital in Frankfurt."

"Home sweet home," Rod muttered. "You can bet he got better treatment than we did."

Thomas thought back to the hospital where he almost lost an arm to amputation. If he hadn't known German, maybe they would have taken it off. He shook his head to clear away the memories of the hospital and turned his thoughts back to General Vannaman. He wondered if the Nazis realized how valuable their captive was.

The general entered the camp, took a quick look at the men, and then continued with his escort to the base commander's office. The men slowly dispersed. They'd find out more about the general later.

◆   ◆   ◆

At the end of August, Thomas wrote Marie requesting "long johns" for the winter. It was still summer, but he guessed he'd be spending Christmas as a prisoner. If the winter was harsh, he wanted to be prepared.

More time passed. The package from Marie came and she'd done exactly as he requested. A pair of "long johns" was included. He carefully packed it away for later.

To the prisoners, the Allies growing superiority over the German Luftwaffe was obvious. The bombings the prisoners witnessed seemed more prolonged. As the *Kriegies* learned more about the success of the invasion and the advancement through France, they began to wonder who would reach them first—the Russians from the east or the Allies from the west.

"Paris has been liberated," Dunn informed the prisoners one night. "The German garrison surrendered. It happened on August 25th."

"How soon? How soon will they be here?" the men asked.

"I don't know. The Russians and the American led forces are making rapid advances. The Russians have taken Bucharest."

Time: Time moved so slowly. Thomas was getting sick of playing chess. He either played chess, attended a band concert at the prisoner's theater, read, or walked the perimeter of the camp. The days had little variation.

When night came and they returned to their quarters, he and the others could hear an occasional air raid in the distance. Some of the raids seemed incredibly close. But they never hit the camp.

Fall came. As it began to be felt in the compound, a new group of airmen prisoners entered Sagan. With their appearance, the prisoners learned the truth about what was happening in the concentration camps.

The 100 airmen who entered the camp on October 21 looked as if they could barely put one foot in front of the other when they were unloaded from the trucks. Thomas couldn't take his eyes off them. Their uniforms hung from their bony shoulders as if they were draped on ill-fitted mannequins.

"What has happened to them?" he asked Rod.

"I don't know," his friend answered. "They look worse than the slave laborers who come here every so often."

The men stood, shocked at the airmen's skeleton-like appearance. A hushed murmur went through the ranks. There was still a semblance of defiance in the eyes of these new prisoners. As Thomas first looked at them, he'd seen the thinness of the men, their gaunt appearance. When he had a chance, he and most of the men gathered around the new arrivals and listened to their story. They sat down in a circle and waited.

"I was shot down in France," one of the men said as he took on the role of spokesman for the others in the group. "I tried to escape through the French underground, but someone betrayed the resistance. The Germans took me prisoner and executed everyone they thought was involved with the underground."

"How many?" Thomas asked.

"I'm not sure. It may have been hundreds."

The man kept rubbing his arm and Thomas looked down at the man's forearm. There was a number on it, a number like you'd put on the flank of cattle.

"You guys don't know how lucky you are. I've been in hell," he said.

"Hell?" Rod asked.

"Buchenwald. A couple of the others here have been in Dachau. They're some of the concentration camps that we'd heard stories about before becoming prisoners."

"Then, the rumors are true?" Thomas asked. His face mirrored his surprise and disbelief.

"The reality is worse than the rumors," the man answered. He looked away before continuing, as if compelled to let those in the camp know what was happening.

"They are killing the Jews, and gypsies, and anyone else who isn't what they think of as a proper Aryan."

One of the prisoners was about to object. Thomas knew what he was thinking. No one could imagine a nation involved in such wholesale slaughter.

"How many are dying?" one of the prisoner's spoke so softly the others could barely hear him.

"Hundreds, thousands, too many," the Buchenwald man responded. He paused, then continued. "The Germans strip them and force them into what they think is a shower. A shower…," he laughed bitterly. "It's no shower. It's a building they fill with gas. Then, after those who are brought into that so-called shower are dead, they burn them in ovens."

"No!" one of the men gasped.

"Yes."

"But no civilized people would stand for it."

"Who said anything about it being civilized," the man said. "It's horrible, brutal murder."

"Do you think the Germans know?" Thomas asked.

"Oh, I don't know if they know specifics. But they must surely guess."

"I'm part German," Thomas protested. "I can't imagine standing by and letting this happen."

The man idly drew a circle in the soil, seemingly oblivious to those around him. Then, he looked up at Thomas, "I couldn't either, until I lived it."

The *Kriegies* were hushed. Trying to take it in, but having difficulty imagining the horror the man described. No more questions were asked. No one wanted more details. They sat and stood around the prisoner as if afraid to speak. Finally, the prisoner stood up and walked away.

It wasn't until then that Thomas noticed that one of the guards was close by, listening. The man, who Thomas knew was a veteran of World War I, looked shocked. His face was pale. The old veteran slowly turned away, walking in the opposite direction.

17

Winter Approaches

It was near the end of October and Thomas already felt the chill in the air. Winter would soon move into Europe. He wondered if it would slow down the Allied advance. It had been rainy and if the temperature dropped much further it could be a miserable winter. He decided not to wait any longer and put on the "long johns" Marie had sent him. Shortly after doing so, the Germans issued heavier coats to the prisoners.

The coat Thomas received was a French coat. It was heavy and warm. However, the coat and the long johns made him keenly aware of the weight he had lost. Normally the winter underwear would cling to his frame. Now it felt like it had too many folds and did not fit him properly. Marie could not have known the situation he and the other *Kriegies* were facing with cutbacks in food distribution. Nor, would he tell her. He and the other POWs didn't want to alarm their families.

He wished there was a solution to the constant hollow feeling he felt. He hadn't had a solid meal in months. Every time he and the other prisoners went outside for the required German inspections in the morning and at night, they were exposed to the changing weather. Rain pummeled the camp and the men during the first few weeks of November. He longed for it to cease and give way to the dry cold he had experienced while in training in Texas.

The Texas weather could be unpredictable and occasionally gave way to a humid cold with storms too. So, maybe he was just making it seem better than it was. Realistically, if the rain ceased, snow might not be far behind. As Thanksgiving approached, he and the other prisoners keenly felt the lack of family companionship. However, all of them knew it would be worse at Christmas.

Thomas thought of Chicago. With Christmas approaching there would be shopping. Even in wartime, the holidays wouldn't be denied. He remembered how festive Marshall Field's windows were and wondered what the theme would be this year. They were always decorated and he and his friends liked the feeling of being transported to another world each Christmas season as they viewed them.

Marie had tried to keep him posted about the family. However, she was limited about what she knew and what she could write him. He didn't know the fate of his brothers. Will was in the Army in Europe. Frederick, the youngest, was a prisoner of the Japanese. Richard was still in the United States, although he had enlisted too. Any news about them would not reach him. He hoped and prayed they were all okay.

No, Marie wouldn't write him about his brothers. Instead, she would try and let him know about events at home that would pass the censors. She had written him about a new movie, Going My Way, with Bing Crosby. The USO had featured him and Bob Hope and some of the jazz bands in England. However, with little to do except read and walk around the camp, the *Kriegies* had established their own bands and even put on dramas. It passed the time and some of the men would spend hours preparing for a performance.

He thought briefly about his walks in the Chicago Loop. The walk he used to take on State Street had given way to the constant walking around the perimeter of the camp. No matter what the weather was, he was determined to be able to withstand a march further into the heart of Germany if the word was given to move the prisoners out. Other *Kriegies* felt the same way. Each day, the same men walked around the camp. There was little else they could do to prepare for what might come. However, hee and the other prisoners still had hopes they would be free by Christmas.

What would the Germans do? That was the question. Some of the men didn't bother exercising. They felt the Germans would not bother trying to move a camp of almost 12,000 men.

"We're a bargaining chip for Hitler," Thomas mentioned to one of the men who sat down by the wooden barracks watching him as he was about to walk around the camp. "Why don't you join me?"

"I'll let you do the walkin', Thomas. There's no bloody way that the Jerries want to have to escort us across Germany. They'll let the Allies or Russians free us. It doesn't matter to them. I'm saving my strength. I'd advise you to do the same."

There was no way he could convince the man otherwise. He'd tried before. Each man had to decide for himself what was best for his own health. None of them knew what the Germans would do if the Allies approached closer to the camp. However, the officers advised them to be ready for the eventuality of a march in inclement weather. So, he would be prepared. He bowed his head against the force of the wind and headed out into the blustery weather.

Would the Germans wait and surrender to the first army that captured the camp? Or, would they march them further into Germany? They couldn't move much closer to Berlin. It was only 60 miles away. Who knew what that mad man, Hitler would do? Thomas shifted his attention to the perimeter of the camp. He fell in step with other *Kriegies* as they sought to keep in shape for what might lie ahead.

In the evening, the men would get reports in their barracks from those who listened to the BBC. Each night they hoped to hear freedom was closer at hand. And, each morning they would wake to another *"appel,"* another count by the Germans to make sure no one had escaped. It was a deadly routine of hope, waiting and routine. There was also a continuing decline in the quality of the food that the Germans provided.

When Thomas swore the meal situation couldn't get worse, it did. The Germans cut back on the food they provided the *Kriegies*. There were still the half parcels sent through the Red Cross, but the lack of other food items made the situation worse. He and the other prisoners began to drop more weight.

Rain was more frequent now. Fortunately, the French coat Thomas was given repelled the November rains. As November wore on, the temperature dropped and the men began to mutter about being dragged out for morning and evening *"appels."*

December came. More rain accompanied its entrance. It was also getting to be bitter cold. Snow started to fall, but it didn't stick. However, it was a constant reminder of what lay ahead. Thomas recalled that the worst of the winter usually hit the Chicago area between January and March. He hoped it wouldn't be that way in Sagan.

Each day the men grumbled at pulling on clothes and stamping outside for another *appel*. The last time news reported from the BBC indicated that the Allies were advancing across a 500-mile front. They had already crossed the Siegfried Line, the main German defensive position. Maybe those who did not take part in the perimeter walking were right. Maybe the camp would be overrun and they'd be set free in days. If they were wrong, he would be prepared for the movement of the camp. So, he kept to his routine. He walked along the fence, in good weather and bad.

The windows of the barracks frosted over because of the cold and only a determined rub removed the ice particles from the glass. Still the men were upbeat.

They knew the Russians were closing in from the East. The allies had already invaded Italy. Germany was caught in between three thrusts.

"I never thought I'd welcome the sight of a Russian army," Thomas said. "But if Uncle Joe's men get here before Christmas, it's fine with me."

"Yep, Uncle Joe may provide a true Christmas gift," Rod laughed.

December 16 dawned. With its arrival came devastating news, the Germans had counter-attacked through the Ardennes. The news spread rapidly through the camp and was duly reported as "a glorious victory" by the German loudspeaker.

"The Germans have advanced quite a bit," Dunn informed the *Kriegies* later that evening. "The BBC says there is a danger that Bastogne might fall."

"No! No!" one of the men said. "They can't lose," the man broke into tears and retreated to his cot. "I want to go home. I want to go home."

The other prisoners looked away. They felt overwhelmed. There was so much hope built on this attack by the Allies. Didn't they control the air? Weren't the Russians rolling across Eastern Europe? The questions swirled back and forth. All the men could do was await further word from the BBC and pray that the German counter offensive was pushed back and defeated.

Then, came word over the BBC of a massacre. "We just got word that the SS took Americans prisoner near Malmedy and executed them," said Dunn as he informed the men of the recent news.

"Do they know who did it?" Thomas asked.

"Yeah, some son-of-a-bitch named Peifer," Dunn muttered.

"They'll pay," Rod muttered. "They'll pay. The Americans won't forget it. Just like the Brits won't forget the execution of the recaptured British prisoners here after that escape attempt."

Day after day, they waited. Snow began to accumulate around the camp. It made the attempt to circle the camp's perimeter more difficult. The snow became slick and the temperature dropped further. Thomas put on extra socks to keep out the cold and protect his feet from frostbite. He clenched his hands in the pockets of the French coat. He had gloves on, but it felt like the cold pierced through the coat, invading stealthily into his gaunt frame.

December 23 loomed cold and clear. When Thomas looked up at the sky, he felt like giving thanks. The miserable weather that had curtailed air support against the Germans was gone. He strode over to the perimeter of the camp to begin his daily circuit of the area.

"The planes will be in the air now. The tide will turn," Thomas said as he walked beside Commander Dunn that day.

"I agree," said Dunn. "But the Jerries are still putting up a fight. It may be days before they're thrown back."

New Year's Day, Jan. 1, 1945 passed. The German attack was beginning to weaken. By January 12, it was clear Hitler's surprise attack had failed. Not only were the Germans retreating, but also the Russians had launched a gigantic attack along the eastern front. Again, hope surfaced among the *Kriegies*.

"It won't be long now," Thomas said. "We weren't freed by Christmas. But it can't be much longer."

"No, it won't," Rod agreed.

Both men looked up at the clear cold sky. Freedom seemed only days away.

18

Death March

January 27th dawned like any other day in camp. It was cold, so cold that the Germans reported it was the worst winter in 50 years. Thomas had no desire to walk around the camp. Even the thought of going out in the bitter cold caused him to shiver. Yet, the guards seemed to think that nothing should shatter the routine of morning *appels*.

"Get up. Get out," Thomas muttered. "The sooner we get it over with, the sooner we can get out of the wind and cold."

The others in the camp agreed. They might shuffle out in good weather, but in weather like this, they hurried out. As they stood, stamping their military shoes in unison to keep warm, rumors raced through the camp.

"They're going to move us." The words were repeated again and again. The *Kriegies* listened to the wind whipping through the camp. They hoped it would bring the sound of advancing tanks and weapons. However, no sound indicated the approach of the Allies.

"They're going to move us. I know it," Steele said through chattering teeth.

"How can they?" another prisoner asked. "Even the guards don't want to be out in this."

Thomas wasn't so sure. Would the Germans prefer getting them out to facing the Russians? He could see the fear in the guards' eyes whenever the Russian front was mentioned. They had no desire to wait for whatever punishment the Russians would wield. The guards also knew the war was over. The counter-offensive against the Allies had been thrust back. It was only a matter of time.

Word circled through the camp that the Allies had passed Sagan on the north and the south.

"They're only about 15 miles away," Rod said.

"They might as well be 200," Thomas said. "Until they get here I'm not going to count on our liberation." He left Steele behind in the cabin after *appel*.

Only a fool would go out when the weather was this cold, he thought. One of the guards said it was 40 below during the mandatory morning count. It felt like it. He dressed as warm as he could and forced himself to go out in the blustery cold. He'd make a quick circuit of the perimeter of the camp and spend the rest of the day inside.

There aren't as many men out today, Thomas thought, as he scanned the camp. Every so often, he'd hear a cough. The cough was here and there among those in the West compound, not enough to cause alarm yet. But it was a clue to the health of the prisoners, a clue that the men were showing more signs of weakness due to the cutbacks in food. Evening came and he and the others huddled inside the barracks trying to keep warm. Then, the word came.

"Get ready to move out," Dunn informed them. "The Germans aren't going to let us fall into the hands of the Allies."

"They're crazy," one of the men said. "They expect us to brave this cold?"

Dunn nodded.

The men gathered their meager possessions. Thomas looked at the letters from Marie, wondering if he should leave them. "Pack up the necessities," Dunn advised. "Travel warm and travel light. Take what food you can. The guards will give us some Red Cross packets."

"Why don't we just take our time?" one of the men asked.

"Delay," another said.

"Delaying may cost a life," Dunn answered. "They'd just as soon get us out and moving. If they spot people trying to delay...," he didn't continue. He didn't have to finish the sentence. The men got his drift.

Thank goodness he had taken part in those walks around the perimeter, Thomas thought. He was in better shape than many in the room. Yet, he, like all the others, had lost weight. How far could he walk in snow and cold?

Some of the men wouldn't be able to last in this weather. They were too weak. Thomas took the scarf Marie sent him and cut it in half, then half again. He took a thread and meticulously sewed the four pieces into mittens. He then took out three pairs of socks. One he'd keep next to his skin to keep it warm and change his socks every night so his feet would at least stay dry. Hopefully the military shoes he and the others had would keep out the wet snow.

The barrack's room had once been quiet as evening descended. No longer. *Kriegies* were frantically trying to assemble packets to carry. Each man packed meat, dried fruit, oatmeal and chocolate. Even those who didn't smoke placed packages of cigarettes in their bundles.

Some of the men, like Thomas, had already donned long underwear. Those who hadn't, donned it now. All of them took a blanket, a towel, some soap, a toothbrush and toothpowder. He watched as men carefully placed packets of letters in their bundles. Others packed as many tins of food as possible, not realizing that with every tin packet they increased the weight of their burdens.

In less than two hours, they formed up into blocks. At a signal, from a German officer, duly relayed by his American counterpart, they approached the gates of the camps. The men formed a column three abreast and followed the path of the other blocks of prisoners toward the entrance to Stalag Luft III. Overhead they could see the prison guards in their wooden watchtowers guns at the ready. Behind them, near the camp theater, another group was forming. Instinctively Thomas knew those men would not accompany them. They were too weak to make the trek. What would happen to them? He turned his attention back to the gate.

A guard went along on either side of the men, counting. Then, the guards signaled them to march through the gates. Before they did, word was passed through the column. "If anyone escapes, two prisoners will be shot."

"What is the point of that?" Thomas muttered. "If anyone leaves the column, he won't last in the cold."

"Tell the goons that, Thomas," Steele said.

"March, March," Dunn ordered. "Just put one foot in front of the other and follow the man in front of you."

The snow was packed and hard as the prisoners ventured forth. They soon discovered that in some areas the snow had turned to ice. The men struggled to keep their balance as they moved forward. The *Kriegies* left the barbed wire of the camp behind them and headed southwest.

Every hour they'd stop for a few minutes. The breaks weren't long enough. As the cold became more intense, it became harder to start moving again. On either side of the road they traversed, was deep snow. Not too far beyond the snowdrifts, were trees swaying back and forth with the wind forming clumps of white on their branches.

Kriegies weren't the only ones abandoning the area around Sagan. Roads were also crowded with refugees fleeing the oncoming Russian troops. These people were farmers. They drove carts crammed with personal belongings. As their horse drawn wagons pushed forward, German guards kept them in a lane separate from the prisoners.

Even the guards were having problems in the snow. They were not the athletic soldiers that Hitler pointed to in his propaganda films. They were not the men with Iron Crosses draped around their necks. Instead, guards in full field packs, plodded forward as if in their own world. They were supposed to be in charge of the prisoners. Thomas couldn't help feeling sorry for some of these 60 year-old veterans from World War I.

Some of the prison guards he disliked. Some of the younger ones had even shot *Kriegies* who had stood at their barrack doors at night when the doors were required to be closed. Older veterans usually did not fall into that group.

"My shoes are beginning to freeze," one *Kriegie* complained as they continued the midnight march.

His words drifted away on the wind. Thomas concentrated on walking and wiggled his toes every so often. He didn't want to have frostbite set in. It was now two in the morning and still they marched. They passed the city of Sagan on the right. They stopped for a rest and the men could hear the rumble of explosions on either side of the column as they continued west.

Thomas began to notice men pulling items from their packs and discarding them in snow banks along the road. Although he was traveling light, his pack seemed to become heavier with each step. Flying boots, letters neatly bound and extra tins littered snowdrifts on either side of the column. He even saw a few of the guards tossing away some of their field pack items.

◆   ◆   ◆

The snow muffled his steps. It seemed like an eternity of marching. He had not expected to remember so much of his life during this unbelievably cold night. Was it the cold that had brought back such vivid memories? Were the others reliving their lives, up to this moment like he had? He'd remembered so much of his past—his life in Bensenville, Marie, the few years at college, the accomplishments and the disappointments, his training as a navigator and his first exposure to enemy fire. All of his memories had seemed to engulf him in the hours of this march.

Sometimes he could feel the snow as it seeped into his boots. He continued hour after hour. At four a.m., it began to snow again. And, still they marched. On either side of them at strategic intervals were some of the German guards with their rifles and machine guns covering the column. One or two of the men sat down beside the road. No amount of coaxing could get them to continue.

"It'll get worse," Thomas said as he walked past. Steele nodded. It took too much energy to talk.

Thomas saw wires swaying back and forth as they approached a snow covered prairie. Electric wires, he thought. As the high tension wires swayed, seemingly ready to burst under the weight of the snow, they gave off a series of bright flaming lights against the dark sky. It was as if they were the lengthening wires of firecrackers. Flame and sparks exploded in the night. Any moment Thomas expected the dipping wires to break and cast their electric flame on the *Kriegies* underneath. All of the men walked forward, close to the wires, mesmerized by their windswept dance.

Why don't they break? he wondered. Then, thanked God when he thought he was beyond their deadly reach, only to see a continuation of the snapping, flame licking at the wires ahead of him.

German civilians alongside the road brought pails of hot water to the men and filled drinking cups. Their journey away from the Allies had taken the exhausted men almost 17 kilometers to the town of Halbau. The *Kriegies* stood in the center of the town for hours, almost ready to collapse.

Finally, they were divided up into groups. Some moved into a church. Thomas and those in his block moved beyond the church to an old barn. His eyes swept over the hay. It reminded him of Bensenville and the days he had spent in that warm, toasty environment. This hay wasn't clean and dry. It was dirty and the wind blew through openings in the walls the farmers used to aerate the hay. Thomas climbed toward the top of the barn, hoping to find a cleaner, warmer area to sleep. Near the top, he stretched out on the hay covering himself with the softness of it.

19

Snow Takes Its Toll

Day one of their march passed into a dim crescendo of marching feet. Thomas could barely move after throwing himself down on the hay. He fumbled at untying the laces to his shoes, finally pulled the shoes off and managed to take his socks off. He could barely bend over to do it, but he knew he couldn't keep wearing the socks. They were wet from perspiration and the damp cold that had seeped into his shoes. He used the hay to dry his feet and somehow remembered to place the socks against his sweating body. Groaning from the effort, he fell back on the hay.

Thomas sank into a deep, dreamless sleep. Many nights in the prison camp he would think about Marie. He would see her face and it would make the days more bearable. But today, he was too exhausted, too tired to even notice those around him. Four hours passed.

Day two began at 8:30 a.m. on the 30th. Thomas remained with the group from block 160. If they kept together, maybe they'd survive the march, he thought. Wind constantly buffeted the men as they strove to keep going. Snow battered them forming miniature white pellets in the freezing weather. Every time Thomas gasped for breath, he felt the pain from the cold he breathed into his lungs. They stopped for a ten-minute break and the marchers began reaching into their packs, trying to rid themselves of anything that seemed too heavy to carry.

Thomas was no exception. He had kept Marie's letters up to this point. It was too much. He couldn't continue with them. Reluctantly he discarded them and some jars of food. He decided to keep the cigarettes in hopes he could trade them for something along the way. He glanced at the other men. Their faces coated with snow, reminded him of walking snowmen. When he was little he'd built snowmen at Bensenville. The thought of that now sent a chill down his spine. The *Kriegies* weren't just walking snowmen. They were walking icemen. The snow soaked into their beards had frozen and formed ice.

The prisoners didn't bother to brush it away. What good would it do? In five more minutes they'd be coated with the blinding snow again.

"Move on!" someone ordered.

The men groaned and moved on following each other on a winding path through the snow. Somewhere beneath the snow there must be a road, Thomas thought. They must be on a road. Roads connect to towns. Maybe they would reach another one and he could rest. Mustn't think of rest, he told himself. If he did, he might be too willing to sit down in the snow banks and freeze to death.

How can we keep going? Thomas wondered. Mile after mile the *Kriegies* and the World War I guards walked. If he had been in the shape he was when he entered the Air Corps he might have barely felt the march. He'd have weather-proof garments. His teeth wouldn't be chattering from the cold and his legs wouldn't feel like they might be going numb. After losing almost 50 pounds in less than a year as a prisoner, he had problems continuing with the snake-like column.

Thomas saw more men stopping now, unable to continue. Sinking into the snowdrifts, they waited for the deathly cold to claim them. He passed one man with tears freezing on his face. He sat in the snow, knowing what it meant and crying at the thought of the cold hand of death.

"Come on, man," Thomas called softly. "You don't want to give in. I can see that."

"I can't go on. I can't even feel my legs anymore," the man responded. "I don't think they're there."

"They're there," Thomas stopped. The man behind him walked into him and cursed him for halting. "Get up. Walk. You'll die here."

The man shook his head.

Thomas looked toward the column that was passing by. He must remain with his group. If he tried to carry the man, he'd not be able to survive. Reluctantly he went on.

"There's nothing you could do for him," Thomas told himself. But he couldn't help looking back. The man was no longer sitting by the side of the road. He had fallen over now and lay still. Thomas watched as snow continued to fall and began to cover the exhausted marcher.

Keep going. Keep going. His feet seemed to march to the beat of those words. He must keep going.

More prisoners fell by the wayside. How many? He didn't know. Maybe the Germans would pick up some. Maybe not.

Another break. Thomas sat down on the icy road, remembering to wiggle his toes. They mustn't get numb. Too soon, they started again. Hour after hour they continued. When would the Germans allow them to rest? At every kilometer, Thomas saw *Kriegies* lying in the snow alongside the road. Was anyone keeping track? How many have we lost on this senseless march?

The agony from the cold was unbelievable. Fitzgerald, the bombardier and Steele continued the shuffling pace. Then, alongside of him, he saw Marc DeCaro sit down.

"Come on, Marc. Don't quit," Thomas called. The slightly built DeCaro shook his head as if trying to block out Thomas' words.

"Marc, give me your pack. If I take your pack, I know you can make it."

DeCaro looked up at Thomas as if he couldn't believe his words.

"Come on, give me the pack," Thomas ordered. He helped Marc take off his pack. It was light, DeCaro had thrown away almost everything he'd packed on the 27th. Yet, he still had trouble continuing in the column.

"It's like we're heading straight to hell, a frozen hell," Marc said. He met Thomas's eyes. "Are you sure you want to do this?"

Thomas grabbed the pack and helped him to his feet.

"Half a league, half-a-league onward," he muttered as he swung the pack to his back alongside his own pack. That was "The Charge of the Light Brigade" into the valley of death. We're facing another kind of death, a death from ice, snow and cold. We're not charging. We're walking into our own version of death. It isn't a glorious charge into the face of death, but a slow, tortuous advance. Each man walking and stumbling in a line with others.

Thomas thought he knew war was hell from the times he flew on his B 17 bomber. He'd seen the burning of targets after the bombs had been dropped. At a high altitude, he wasn't closely involved. He'd been shot down and seen the damage the bombs did in the cities. He'd also seen the military prisoners who'd been sent to the concentration camps. He'd heard their tales of the beastly slaughter of Jews and anyone else who happened to be against the Nazis. But, he'd never truly walked so closely with death as now. Being in a plane, being shot down, it was something that happened to soldiers. But this? This was not anything he expected.

The prisoners came upon more farms and barns. The Germans again herded the *Kriegies* into the barns. Thomas slumped to the barn's floor. The second day of marching had ended. He was still alive. Would he be able to survive a third day? He would and he could. He barely looked around the barn this time. He was too exhausted.

Thomas knew the other prisoners felt the same as he did. He could tell from their whimpers and moans. Then there was the absolute quiet of the men. He didn't even bother to open his pack and look for food. The Germans hadn't distributed any to the prisoners since they started. Everyone, even the guards were weak from the effort. No food, hardly any water. The *Kriegies* collapsed where they fell. If the Russians were two miles away, the prisoners wouldn't have heard them.

On the third day, the prisoners again formed a column to continue the march. At 0600 hours, the men went forth. This time the weather was a little warmer. Instead of the snow pelting them during the day, they now slipped in the slush made by thousands of feet. It wasn't just slush. Ice had formed from the constant movement of the *Kriegies* on the melting snow. Now they fell, dragged themselves up from the icy surface. Continuing. Continuing.

Thomas lost track of time. He just concentrated on placing one foot in front of another. His whole body ached, ached from carrying his pack and helping others with theirs. The sleds that some of the men used to pull their supplies were useless. They caught repeatedly in the slush formed as the temperature rose. The prisoners pulling them finally gave up.

More and more items were abandoned on either side of the slush-covered road. Items deemed too heavy were cast aside. Thomas knew the only thought of the *Kriegies* was survival. Stay alive now. Worry about tomorrow later.

Was this the second or third day of marching? He was losing track. Hours later, they reached another stopping point. The sun moved lower in the sky and still they marched. There were fewer breaks. Every so often Thomas passed another *Kriegie* lying on the side of the road. Each time, he turned his eyes away, not wanting to know who he was. Could the man be from Chicago? Could he be someone he knew? He didn't dare find out.

"Oh God, help me," he whispered.

"Did you say something Thomas?" Rod asked.

Thomas had almost forgotten the copilot was nearby.

"I only asked for help," Thomas said.

"You and everyone else on this death march," Rod sighed. "I swear if I live through this I'm not going to take life for granted any more."

Darkness came and the Germans guided them into another town, Muskau. This time Thomas and the other *Kriegies* found themselves in a pottery factory. It was filthy, but it was dry and warm. When Thomas, Rod and some of the other men entered the factory, they found the first floor already filled with prisoners who'd arrived before them.

Thomas and some of the other men wearily climbed up to a balcony extending out from the second floor. It was warmer than the first floor because it was nearer where the soot settled from the furnaces. When he finally lowered himself to the floor, his hand sank into three or four inches of black ashes and soot. But he didn't care. All he wanted to do was lie down and rest. He barely remembered to take his shoes and socks off and placed the sweaty, wet pair of socks next to his body. They'd dry and he'd put them on in the morning.

Too tired. Too very tired. He grimaced in pain, then fell asleep.

20

Fatal Journey

Thomas slept, but during the night he dreamt about the journey to Muskau. Again and again, he saw the men stumble forward, then fall, as they tried to stay alive. As he relived the march and its agony, he again saw the men sitting or lying beside the route, waiting to die. It was an endless nightmare. It repeated and repeated itself. He'd wake up thinking he was still marching in the endless column.

He'd look around the factory for a second or two, seeing the other *Kriegies* lying almost on top of each other like "pick up sticks." However, they weren't sleeping soundly. They were tossing and turning. Occasionally there would be a moan or whimper, and he guessed that they too were reliving the journey from Sagan.

The concrete floor of the factory made his muscles ache. Still, it was somewhat warm inside away from the elements. Thomas could hear the wind blowing against the building. It didn't seem as strong or threatening as the night of the march. Nothing would ever be as threatening as that march. He knew he would never forget it.

He closed his eyes, willing sleep and rest might find him. But as soon as sleep entered on darkened wings, he was transported back in his dreams to the hills outside of Muskau. He saw the men he'd passed during the march, lying in the snow banks, waiting for death. He wanted to scream at them. Get up! Don't give up! But he knew it was useless.

In the morning on February 1, word trickled through the camp the Germans would allow them to rest a day before continuing.

Thank God, he thought. He was stronger than some of the men. If they had continued marching without rest, he questioned whether he'd survive. As he sat and occasionally rubbed his aching legs, Thomas heard snatches of description of the march and the blizzard.

"The South Barracks really had it bad. They were the first group out breaking the trail for the rest of us," someone said.

The 2000 men of the South, what an ordeal to plow through roads covered with snow, Thomas thought.

"Yeah, but those left on the road came from every barracks," another said.

Every barracks! How could the Germans force half-starved men to venture forth in the worst blizzard in 50 years? He'd never understand that. Even the old guards suffered because of the idiot who ordered this.

"There were 11,000 of us moving south from Sagan," a third prisoner added.

Thomas heard Dunn's voice in the background. Then the words filtered through, "At least 2000 didn't make it."

"Two thousand!" several men gasped. "That's a fifth of the prisoners."

"Yes, maybe more," another said

Thomas looked in the direction of the conversation, wondering. Could what the men said be true? Could that many have died? He tried to remember how many he had seen dead or dying alongside the column. Then, he gave up. His mind was too numb to think about it.

Silence swept through the factory. Thomas could see that the men were having difficulty grasping the enormity of the disaster. Then, a stirring at the doors of the factory broke the silence.

"They're going to feed us!" a *Kriegie* called.

Thomas and the other *Kriegies* scrambled to their feet and started to move toward the entrance. Then, he heard Dunn's voice again.

"No use going out in the cold. We'll just stand around waiting. Take a section at a time. The men grumbled, then sat down and waited. Group after group made their way to the doors and returned to their places with hard bread and a Red Cross parcel to be split among groups of six.

This was the first food the *Kriegies* had received since leaving Sagan. Three days with little or no food, except for what they scrounged from their own packs and water gleaned from melted snow. The prisoners greedily devoured the bread and small portions of food from the Red Cross parcel. Thomas and some of the other prisoners traded cigarettes for pickled beets and potatoes to supplement the meager allotment.

The Germans allowed them to rest. However, during the early dawn hours, on the third of February the march resumed. Glausteen was their next destination. As Thomas and the other *Kriegies* left the shelter of the factory, he noticed the snow had finally stopped falling and it was melting rapidly

Thomas nudged him. There was no response. Suddenly he realized the man was dead. He motioned to Dunn and pointed at the *Kriegie*. Dunn nodded and shook his head.

"If we get to stop, we'll get him out of here, Thomas," he said.

By now, several other prisoners were in the same condition. By common consensus, the *Kriegies* eased them toward the door. Hours later the train stopped and the doors were thrown open. Some took time to drop their dead comrades from the train. Others rushed out to relieve themselves as the guards watched.

They continued on by train, reaching Cemnitz on the fifth. As they stood waiting in the cars, a siren sounded.

"Air raid!" someone called out. Thomas and the others could feel the ground shaking around them. Hearing the whine of bullets, the men cowered against each other.

"Let us out of here," someone screamed.

"Please, let us out," another begged.

There was no response.

"The guards must have taken shelter," Thomas whispered.

"Yeah," another *Kriegie* said. "And we're left like sitting ducks."

An occasional whimper could be heard from the prisoners. Finally, someone yelled at the man to shut up. The train started up again. Thomas wondered if any *Kriegies* had died during the raid. If they did, then that was more that the goons would have to account for when the war was over. To leave them trapped as they had, with no chance to flee the attack was criminal.

It was now February 6. The train made another stop at Zwickau and proceeded toward Nuremburg on the seventh.

21

Arrival at Nuremberg

It was a short walk from the rail yard to the prison at Nuremberg. Yet, the walk seemed to take forever. Thomas felt as if he could barely put one foot in front of the other. He guessed he must have lost ten pounds while being transported by boxcar. How many days was he confined in that car? Two, three days? He felt weak, incredibly weak. All he wanted to do was collapse when he entered the barbwire enclosure. He couldn't. The guards insisted on assigning the men to barracks. What did he care what barracks he was in? All he wanted to do was lie down and sleep.

After they were assigned to barracks by the guards, they stumbled toward their new prison homes. As they approached, Thomas noticed something different from the prison at Sagan. Sagan was kept clean. The prison at Nuremberg literally stank. Open latrines gave an overwhelming odor to those who approached them. They were too close to the barracks Thomas thought as he gingerly avoided them and entered the crowded wooden barracks. Inside, were straw mattresses alive with lice, bedbugs and vermin. The bugs seemed to move like a horde of small soldiers overrunning a battlefield.

What was the battlefield? Thomas didn't even want to consider them as part of the war. Yet there they were. He saw mice scurrying around. It didn't matter now. He threw a blanket down on the straw and collapsed. Then he felt the nip of the critters that had made the dirty mattresses their home. He wanted to crawl out of the bed and go outside, but he was too weak and tired.

"I'll go outside tomorrow," he told himself before falling asleep.

The following morning he woke up, covered with bites. He got up and went outside. It was then he learned that Italians had once been incarcerated in the prison. They had stripped the place of practically all the wood in the camp. Even the wood from the toilets were removed for firewood in an attempt to keep warm over the winter.

The Italians were gone, but not forgotten. They left behind the remnants of the building to the next prisoners. Thomas looked around the crowded camp in disgust. He tried to ignore the filthy conditions. His main objective now was to find something to eat.

"Where do we get our rations?" Thomas asked a fellow prisoner.

"What rations?" the prisoner spat. "If you find Red Cross parcels here let me know."

"They can't just put us here without any provisions!" Thomas said, hoping that the man was wrong. He looked at the man. His uniform was dirty and unkempt, his hair stringy and his face unshaven. As he took in the man's appearance, he realized that the man smelled.

"Am I as bad as that?" he wondered. This man has been degraded so anyone who approached him would shy away from the dirty prisoner of war. Thomas staggered away, hoping to find a place where he could just sit. At Sagan he had made a point of walking around the perimeter of the camp to keep in shape. Now, all he wanted to do was stay in the open, by the fence and await rescue by the Allied forces.

In the days that followed, the Germans did manage to provide the *Kriegies* with a piece of hard bread and some soup. Thomas would stumble to the line for food, then return to his chosen place by the fence. No Red Cross parcels came. He could almost feel the weight dropping from his frame. He felt weaker and weaker.

The first night he was forced into slit trenches by the guards when the RAF flew over to bomb the nearby railroad-marshaling yard. After that first night, they stood outside the barracks and watched the attack.

"Have they ever hit the camp?" Thomas asked during that first night.

"No," a prisoner replied. "Watch during the very beginning of the next attack and you'll see why."

Thomas watched as the planes came over during another attack. It was then that he saw the flares.

"They mark the camp every night before dropping their bombs," the prisoner that he had spoken to on the previous night explained. "Every corner of the camp is marked and they never bomb within those flares.

"Thank you, RAF," Thomas exclaimed.

The two prisoners stood together watching the flash of bombs in the distance. As the sound of explosions ripped through the night, Thomas and the other *Kriegies* counted. "One thousand one, one thousand two...."

They didn't get far in their count before the flames from the explosions lit up the night sky. One evening they watched as the searchlights of the Germans locked on an RAF bomber. A few seconds later, there was a plume of smoke trailing from the plane and it began to lose altitude.

Thomas wondered if there would be any survivors from the hit plane. He recalled how little time he had to bail out when he was shot down. The bomber appeared to steady itself and he thought he saw a parachute against the night sky. A short while later the plane disappeared from view.

The following morning, the guards brought in more prisoners. The *Kriegies* soon learned the prisoners were from the plane shot down the night before. Attack on the rail yard occurred during day and night. Thomas felt thankful he and the other prisoners had arrived before this series of attacks. If they hadn't, they might have been locked in the rail cars, sitting ducks for the oncoming planes.

As the month of March approached, the food continued to be inadequate. Clothing to replace worn uniforms was non-existent. Unlike Sagan, the prisoners had no coal to heat the barracks. Even the wood was gone, commandeered by the previous tenants of the prison, the Italians. Would any Red Cross parcels ever get through? Thomas wondered.

If there were any, he and the other *Kriegies* saw no sign of them. As he and the others waited, the camp became a breeding ground for disease. Three weeks after their arrival at Nuremberg, some Red Cross parcels finally arrived. They were quickly exhausted as the starving men tried to parcel them out so every one would have something to eat. But there were too few. It was almost as if none had arrived. The continuing lack of clean dishes and being held at night in the barracks with only a can to be passed among the men so they could relieve themselves began to have an effect.

More men were collapsing from the starvation rations. Diarrhea and dysentery spread through the camp. Thomas began to wonder if the weakened condition of the men would expose them to influenza or worse. He came down with dysentery. It became an agony for him at night in the vermin-infested barracks. He had been free of illness while at Sagan, except for the wound when he was shot down and the carbuncles. This time he wasn't so fortunate. He and many of the others now suffered from diarrhea. As his health deteriorated, he wondered for the first time if he would survive the war.

"If only we had the means to even clean this rat hole, it might save lives," he said. "But I don't see the Jerries doing a thing. Individual bars of soap are useless."

April approached and with it the weather began to moderate. Thomas and the other *Kriegies* continued to hope the Allies would reach them within days. But, again, their hopes for freedom were dashed. They received word they would be moved to Moosberg during the first week of April.

"*Appel. Appel*" rang through the camp. As the prisoners formed up as best they could, the German guards fell in beside them at strategic intervals, escorting them out the barbwire gate and south. There was no hurry. It was springtime and warm. As the men marched to the south, they stopped after 13 miles at the town of Neumarkt.

"We're fertilizing the country as we go," Thomas remarked to the prisoner on his right. "Yes. And we'll leave our mark all the way to Munich," the man answered.

22

Near the End

Neumarkt had not been touched by the war as much by the war as Nuremberg or Sagan. There were no prisoner of war camps. As the *Kriegies* approached the village of less than 18,000, Thomas saw a peaceful town nestled in the heart of a wooded valley. When he and the other prisoners entered the town, he sensed a change of attitude among the Germans. There was not the hostility apparent on the faces of the town's people that he had seen in other German towns when he first became a prisoner. Rod Steele nudged him.

"They know they've lost the war," Rod said.

Thomas agreed. However, there was something else about the village that he had not seen in the towns where war damage shattered lives and buildings. There was a sense of "at last it's over." The atmosphere was not only apparent among the villagers. It was there with the old soldiers escorting them south.

The guards were more relaxed during the journey south, letting the *Kriegies* march in groups of ten or twelve at a leisurely pace. Every so often there was a reminder of the fear that pervaded the old guards' ranks. A rumor of approaching Gestapo would send them scurrying to get the prisoners moving faster. It seemed as if the guards were particularly concerned about the prisoners' journey through Neumarkt.

The *Kriegies* wanted to walk slowly to accommodate those who were on the verge of collapsing. With every step, the prisoners remembered the march out of Sagan with its deadly cold, the ride in the boxcars, the dysentery and the lack of food that gnawed at them during the march.

How many miles had they covered? Thomas wondered. Six hundred? It seemed like that. One of the worst situations experienced by the *Kriegies* was at the filthy Nuremberg prison. Thomas remembered this as he half-surveyed the village. Near the center of town, an all too familiar scent wafted through the air.

Beer!

He hadn't had a beer since his days in England. Even then, it was not the pungent scent of good, brown ale. It was like a magnet, drawing the weary prisoners toward what appeared to be a beer garden.

Ah. What he wouldn't give for a beer. The other *Kriegies* began to sidle over toward the beer *stube*. They tried to convince the guards to let them stop.

"Come on!" one *Kriegie* said.

"What harm will it do?" another asked the guard next to him.

"You know we can't allow it," the guard answered. "Move on."

Thomas looked longingly at the chairs and tables outside the beer *stube,* then toward the guards who were coming together to prevent an assault on the tavern by the American prisoners. Holding their guns at the ready, they forced the *Kriegies* to keep marching.

Someday, someday, I'll be back and no one's going to prevent me from having a beer, Thomas told himself. He stumbled along on the right side of the column, past the inviting scent and on through the town. As they continued south, he marveled how nice the weather was. January had been a horror of cold and snow. April was everything it should be, warm, yet not too warm. A gentle reminder that summer would be there in a few months.

Just outside Neumarkt, Thomas and the prisoners heard the sound of motors and saw a bunch of P51s and P47s diving down toward the column, strafing the line of *Kriegies*. Thomas heard cries and shouts. The men dove down on the ground to escape the bullets. The planes circled around and came in again. When the prisoners caught sight of them, they scattered, leaping into ditches near the road. Prisoners landed on top of each other and a German guard jumped down into the ditch beside the men.

"They'll be back," Rod said. "We've got to let them know who we are."

"Let's strip off any spare clothes and blankets in our packs and spell out who we are on the fields," Fitzgerald said.

"Was any one hit?" Thomas asked.

"I think a few, but I don't know if anyone was killed," Steele said.

Then word reached the men that a sergeant had been killed.

The men quickly placed bits and pieces of clothing and blankets on the fields near the road, spelling out the letters, P O W. Now, all they could do was hope the fighter pilots would understand the message.

When the fighters came back, Thomas hugged the earth by the road, praying the pilots would see the letters, praying that they would understand the column they saw were not German fighters but prisoners of war. He and the other *Kriegies* watched and waited.

The planes seemed to be readying to make another swooping dive at the column. However, they must have seen the letters. They circled once and wiggled their wings before leaving.

"Thank God," Thomas said. "They'll pass the word on to any other planes in the area."

The men climbed back on the road as the German guards again drew alongside of them, escorting them along the highway toward the south. As the men from West Camp continued traversing the narrow highway, inching their way south, they marched three abreast. The *Kriegies* numbered two or three thousand men. The slow moving column stretched out for a mile. While the prisoners continued on the trek with little or nothing in their makeshift packs, the elderly guards trudged along beside them with 40 pounds of gear plus their rifles. It was obvious to Thomas and the other men from Luft III West that the guards were tired.

"They're having trouble putting one foot in front of another," Thomas told Rod.

"Yeah. I know. A couple of guys are even carrying their rifles."

"Time to take a rest," Thomas told the guard next to him.

"Ya," the guard acknowledged and sat down on the grass and removed his pack. He began rubbing his neck and shoulders and grimaced.

Thomas's group stopped at a farmhouse near Berching and traded some soap for a domestic rabbit.

"Your wife will kill the rabbit and make some stew," Thomas told the farmer.

"Agreed," the farmer said as he reached for two bars of soap. It took almost three hours for the stew to be prepared. As they waited, Thomas and a few of the men stretched out beneath a tree whose spring leaves were just beginning to burst forth. A guard stayed with them and fussed about the delay.

"We should move on," the guard said.

"Why?" Thomas asked.

"Gestapo," he answered.

"The stew's almost ready," Thomas said. "When we've eaten we'll move on."

The guard walked away while the men sat around enjoying the meal the farmer's wife had prepared. She'd even provided some bread. It was the best meal Thomas had had in a year. He thought seriously of just falling asleep under the tree and letting the night catch up with him.

"We probably should move on," Rod said. "Maybe the Gestapo are close."

"Well, it's them or the retreating Germans. Who's worse?" Thomas asked.

"The Gestapo," Rod answered with no hesitation.

Thomas reluctantly got to his feet. The thought of spending the night sleeping under the tree vanished. As the men continued to move south, they crossed some cold streams and took the time to catch a drink and then wash themselves as best they could.

It was getting warmer. The Germans now allowed the prisoners to move at their own pace. Thomas stopped briefly at another farmhouse and traded his French overcoat for some more food.

"I need a note to go with this coat," the farmer said. "If the Americans come and see this coat, they may shoot me for having it."

"Okay, I will write the note," Thomas said.

The farmer gave him a piece of paper and he wrote, "I traded this coat to this farmer for certain food stuffs on my way south."

At another farmhouse, Thomas stripped off the long underwear he'd worn for the past several months and traded it for some more food. The guards decided they had walked long enough and found a barn to stay in over night. Outdoor fires were forbidden and the men settled for a cold evening meal.

In the morning they had what leftovers remained in their Red Cross parcels and moved on. They would be reaching the Danube soon. Before they did, Thomas and the others came to a crossroads. He looked at the road and said to Rod Steele who was standing next to him, "There's a little church down this roadway."

"I don't see a church," Rod said.

"Well, there is one."

"I thought you'd never been this way before, Thomas," one of the *Kriegies* said.

"I haven't. But, there's a church, a Catholic church. It's about a mile-and-a-half down that road," Thomas said. "Let's go take a look at it."

Rod looked at Thomas for a long moment. It was as if he wanted to ask him, 'How do you know?' Yet he didn't ask.

How did he know? Thomas wondered. Yet he knew. There was a church. It was as if he knew the area, even though he had never been there before. At least I've never been here before in this lifetime, he thought.

This lifetime? What was he thinking? Could he have really been here in another life? That was impossible.

The soldiers did not question him further. They accepted his assurance that there was a church as a matter of course. They had been together through so much that even if there was no logical reason for a church to be where Thomas said, they accepted his assurance that there was a church a short trek away. The group turned down the road with a guard bringing up the rear.

Thomas led the small group along the road. With each step, he was more certain of the existence of the church. But, how did he know? He didn't know how he knew. He just knew it was there. Meanwhile, the *Kriegies* followed him without questioning him further. A mile-and-a-half later a small stone church appeared to their view, right where he had said. It had a small bell tower.

"There's a monastery there. If we ask, they'll give us some food and let us wash ourselves. The church serves the farmers in this area," Thomas said.

Rod looked at Thomas and again asked, "How did you know?"

"I just knew," Thomas said.

The nuns allowed the prisoners to enter a small courtyard. Just as Thomas had envisioned, they distributed food and allowed them to wash up.

"You must move on," a nun with a thick German accent told him in English. "We are afraid."

"Of the Gestapo?"

She nodded and looked furtively at the guard escorting them.

The *Kriegies* finished eating and thanked the nuns for their hospitality. Then, they returned to the trail leading to Moosburg. Fitzgerald brought up the rear, followed by the guard. The men were now approaching the town of Neustadt. Before they reached it, they had to cross the blue Danube. The bridge was blown out and Thomas and the others waded through two feet of water on the sunken bridge. When the prisoners came close to Neustadt they stopped at a farmhouse for the night and traded cigarettes for a cake.

Thomas noticed more German military and civilians as they moved deeper into Bavaria. He guessed they must have walked nearly 100 kilometers. Again, they halted outside of a town and prepared what little food they had left.

The following day the Red Cross reached them with food parcels. It was the first rations the prisoners received since leaving Nuremburg. Thomas estimated they must be a day away from arrival at Moosburg and wondered what the new camp would be like.

The members of West Camp must be the last arrivals at the camp, he thought.

The guards gave the impression that all of the prisoners from Sagan were being centrally located in the one camp.

Thomas and the other prisoners reached Moosburg the following day. As he surveyed the camp, he couldn't believe the number of men on the other side of the prison's gates.

"The Germans must have taken all the prisoners to this location," Thomas said as he observed the camp. Then, the guards motioned them forward and they entered the barbed wire gate to Stalag VIIA, Moosburg.

As he entered the gates, Thomas saw buildings that looked like stucco.

"They look okay from the outside," Rod said.

"But how can so many men stay in those buildings?" Thomas asked.

"We'll find out soon enough," Rod said. When the men from West Camp entered Moosburg, it was as if a small wave had joined an ocean. It seemed as if all the prisoners captured by the Germans throughout the war were in the crowded camp.

23

Eve of Freedom

Thomas soon learned that the dilapidated barracks at Moosburg was built to house 14,000 men. He estimated that the camp now had a population ten times that amount. Some of the barracks had dirt floors. Others consisted of two wooden buildings with a center pathway housing a masonry washroom and a limited kitchen area. When he stepped inside the barracks, he saw tiers of wooden bunks in blocks of 12, built up toward the ceiling. Facilities meant to house 200 prisoners, housed 500.

Before he could find a bunk, the Germans insisted that they shower and be deloused. Thomas and the others stripped, he was shocked at the ribs and bones of his fellow prisoners. As he stared at his fellow *Kriegies,* he realized that if they were skin and bones, he must look the same to them.

The shower was quick and they scrambled into their tattered clothes and headed toward one of the barracks. When Thomas entered the stifling quarters, he found little light. The manner of the placement of the wooden beds showed him a facility equivalent to a crowded urban slum building. It was almost as if the prisoners were stacked in tight quarters, one on top of another. Although he couldn't see the bugs and vermin infesting the barracks, he knew they were there.

One of the first things he had done on entering the camp was to find a latrine. Dysentery was rampant throughout the camp. Some of the *Kriegies* couldn't make it to the aborts or latrines and he had to pick his way through the area to reach the facility to relieve himself. He felt completely exhausted and decided to find a bunk, any bunk, and lie down.

His sleep was fitful and the next morning he found his back covered with bites from the bugs infesting the barracks. As weak as he felt, however, there was something that still was routine in this other prison camp that was similar to his experiences in Sagan, the two-a-day *appels.* Each morning and evening the Germans counted the prisoners to make sure none was absent.

How can they even make an accurate count? Thomas wondered. No one knows, for sure, how many died on that "death march." Still, the Germans insisted upon the *appel* routine even as the war neared its end.

Some of the *Kriegies* decided to stay outside rather than face the bug infested quarters. It was near the end of April. Thomas had been a prisoner of the Germans almost a year. The trip from Neumarkt had given him a chance to trade for fresh food. However, he had only gained a few pounds during that march. The diarrhea made it almost impossible to gain more.

"I must weigh about 120 pounds," Thomas said to a companion from the march from Nuremberg, Barney Swinburne.

"Yeah, we're all in the same boat," Barney said. "The condition we're in doesn't prove a threat to anyone. I don't think the Jerries expect anyone to make a break. We haven't the strength."

Thomas's uniform hung from his gaunt frame. He had to cinch up his trousers so they wouldn't slide down. His cheeks were sunken and his eyes burned. If only he could build up his strength. The Red Cross parcels helped, but they weren't enough to gain back the sixty or seventy pounds he had lost since becoming a guest of Hitler.

After spending one night in the barracks, Thomas moved outside. At least the April weather would provide some warmth. He couldn't have stayed out there if there was any hint of a freak winter storm. During the days that followed he watched the sky around Moosburg fill with Allied planes both day and night. There were no German planes to stop them and they came and went with impunity.

For several days, he and the other *Kriegies* could hear machine gun fire and artillery in the distance. The guards left at the camp were at a minimum, but they were armed and there was always the fear of the Gestapo. Even the guards were afraid of the Gestapo.

On the third day, in the compound, as Thomas sat by the barbed wire fence near one of the gates, he thought he heard cannon fire in the distance.

"The Americans are close," he said to Barney. "Can't you hear the guns?"

Swinburne smiled. Then, Rod Steele joined them.

"I hear the SS has sworn to fight to the death," Rod said.

"I heard the same thing," Thomas acknowledged. "But the old guards have had it. They want to surrender."

"Do you think the SS will let them?" Barney asked.

"The war's over. Why not surrender?" Thomas asked.

The 27th of April came and the sound of gunfire seemed closer.

On the 28th, word spread through the camp that the SS had killed some of the guards who wanted to surrender.

"How could they do that to their own countrymen?" Barney asked.

"Well, we heard some of what they are capable of doing from those 100 men held in concentration camps that the Luftwaffe brought to Sagan," Thomas said. "Does anything they do surprise you?"

"I couldn't believe one human being could do that to another," Barney said.

Thomas looked around the camp. The men might be sick and skin and bones, but there was a glimmer of hope in their eyes. So, they waited. When would they taste freedom? Everyone knew it would be soon. It had to be.

On Sunday, the 29th, at 10 or 11 a.m. there was a rumble of wheels and tread outside the barbed wire. Thomas looked over and saw an American tank rolling over the wire surrounding the compounds of the prison camp. He heard a rattle of shots and looked toward the town of Moosberg.

The SS had taken refuge in a church steeple. Instead of firing at the tank, they began spraying the camp with machine gun fire. Thomas and the other prisoners dove to the ground trying to keep out of the way of the bullets. He wished there was a trench he could dive into and pull the top over to protect himself.

The only trench nearby was the latrine trench. Despite their fear, no man would suffer the added indignity to diving into it. All he could do was hug the ground while the bullets flew past. He heard some of the *Kriegies* crying out in pain, as the lead tore through their arms and legs.

"Trust the SS to pick the easiest target, those with no weapons," Thomas said to two or three men around him.

He inched his way toward the tank. It seemed as if others in the camp had the same idea. When they reached the tank, they pointed toward the steeple. The crew of the armored vehicle swiveled its turret around, unlimbered the cannon and with one shot blew the steeple tower off the church.

The rest of the German guards surrendered.

Thomas stood there tears running down his face. He couldn't believe the moment had come at last. He was free. He'd be going home to Marie. He looked toward a pole where the Nazi flag had flown minutes before. That flag was gone and the American flag flew in its place.

"That is the most gorgeous sight I've ever seen," Thomas sobbed and like the other prisoners, began hugging each other. A slow crescendo built to a roar of approval as the soldiers in the tank appeared. They threw chocolate to the prisoners. Those who caught it immediately stuffed the entire bar in their mouths. A moment later these same prisoners rushed to the latrines. Their stomachs couldn't take the rich chocolate. Thomas was more fortunate. He took only a small piece, savoring the richness of the confection. He sucked on it and then allowed himself to swallow the piece. The rest he put away until later.

The former prisoners didn't know what to do next. They crowded around the one tank and others that soon appeared. Some of the men hugged and kissed their liberators. Thomas stood close to the tanks and heard the comments of the crews.

"Look at these men," one said. "They're like skeletons."

"Not as bad as the concentration camps though," another observed.

"Yeah, but they sure look like their next of kin," a third said.

Are we that bad? Thomas wondered. He looked down at his torn uniform. It was filthy. He hadn't been able to keep himself clean. The soap he had brought along did little good when there was barely enough water to drink. How would he ever get back to what he once was? Would Marie even recognize this shrunken, disheveled navigator? He felt the tears beginning to trickle down his cheeks. He had so much to go home to and yet he didn't want her or his brothers to see him like this.

Three days later the troops under General Patton left the camp. Thomas knew they would have to continue in pursuit of any of the Germans still fighting, but they just took off, leaving the *Kriegies* to their own devices.

"Men, we have plenty of Red Cross parcels. We just need to stay put," one officer said.

The men were in no mood to wait. They scavenged the country looking for fresh meat, potatoes, vegetables, anything that they could bring back to add to the larder of the camp. When they went to a farm they'd ask, how many chickens do you have? How many potatoes? How much cabbage?

If the farmer answered, "None," and the prisoners found food, they would take it all. If the farmer answered honestly, the *Kriegies* took half of what he had back to camp.

The camp took on the appearance of a gigantic harvest celebration. Though they found food in this manner, Thomas and the others were aware their fresh food supply was limited. They needed to be moved to a camp that could accommodate them, a camp that could also take care of their medical needs.

One day, Thomas went into town and found a warehouse stocked with items confiscated by the Germans. He guessed that some of the items had once belonged to the Jewish people taken to the concentration camps, but there was no way of telling for sure. He decided that he would liberate a set of pewter cups and an urn that matched them. After carrying them around for several days, he started giving them away.

"They're too heavy," he told Barney.

"I don't think I'd want anything to remind me of this place," Barney said.

Thomas had to agree. Why did he take the cups and urn anyway? He didn't want to remember what he had been through in Sagan, during the death march, at Nuremberg and here at Moosburg.

Eventually the officers regained control of the camp.

"There's diehard Germans out there," several officers said. "Within a week or two planes will come and take us out of here. They'll take us to a Luftwaffe air base and then fly us to Camp Lucky Strike. That's our ticket home."

24

Kriegies No More

Freedom, what did it mean? Did it mean waiting? Thomas wondered. What are we going to do now? One hundred thousand prisoners stranded at a camp with only promises of food. They were still half-starved. But at least they had food from the Red Cross. It was like being close to an oasis, shimmering in the sunlight as the *Kriegies* approached, but not quite available to quench their thirst.

One day as several of the *Kriegies* sat near their tent trying to heat some of their Red Cross items, a chaplain from a nearby combat engineering unit approached Barney Swinburne and Thomas.

"Where are you fellows from? he asked.

"I'm from Chicago," Thomas said.

"I'm from Cleveland, Ohio," Barney answered.

"I have a church in Cleveland," the minister said as he looked over the men. "What are your names?"

After they told him, he spoke directly to Barney. Is your dad also a minister of a church in Cleveland?"

Barney nodded. Then, added, "Yes, Cleveland seems far away now."

The chaplain studied the crowded tent, the half-starved prisoners and the efforts the prisoners were making to heat the food in makeshift cans before responding. He seemed to be lost in thought.

"Cleveland seems very far away after all this," he finally acknowledged.

"Will you tell my dad I'm safe?" Barney asked. "I've had no chance to write him since the Germans put us here."

"Of course," the chaplain said. "Why don't both of you come back with me to our unit? We'll clean you up and feed you."

"I'm not sure we can get a pass to leave," Thomas said. "You willing to try, Barney?"

"Sure, what good are we doing here?"

"If you'll wait, Chaplain, I'll see if I can get a pass for us."

Thomas went to one of the officers and explained that they had a chance of joining a unit nearby.

"You know the rules, Thomas," the officer said. "We're supposed to stay together. There are die-hard Germans out there and when that unit moves on to Czechoslovakia or wherever Patton's troops are, what are they going to do with you?"

"We're willing to take our chances, sir. We don't know when they'll be sending people here to get us out."

"The answer is still, No."

Thomas walked away, frustrated. He could see the captain's point. However, this chaplain wasn't going to abandon them. He was sure of that. Returning to the chaplain and Barney, he relayed the response."

They say we have to remain here. Your unit could be gone at any time and then what would we do."

"Well, we wouldn't just leave you like the rest of the Army has until now," the chaplain answered. "I'll get you out of here, tomorrow. Just be ready."

After the chaplain left, Thomas and Barney discussed the situation. "Do you think he'll be back?" Barney asked.

"Yes, I think so," Thomas answered. "Tomorrow isn't so far away. We don't have to worry about packing a lot," he laughed. Neither man had much of anything to take with them, although Thomas still retained a few of the pewter cups that he'd liberated from the town warehouse.

The next day the chaplain returned in an ambulance with some medics that were helping the other prisoners. He walked over to the two *Kriegies*.

"Come on. I've got two extra Red Cross helmets. Get in the ambulance and we'll go right out the front gate."

"Yes, sir!" Barney and Thomas said in unison as they stumbled over to the ambulance. They took the proffered helmets and climbed into the back of the vehicle. At a signal from the chaplain, the ambulance driver turned the vehicle around and drove out through the entrance of the camp.

As Thomas looked back at Moosburg from the ambulance, he couldn't believe he was actually leaving the prison camp. He had been a prisoner of the Germans nearly a year. During that time he had lost almost sixty pounds and he was now a shadow of his former self. As the camp faded into the distance, he couldn't help wiping a tear from his eye.

Thomas glanced at Barney from the corner of his eye. He could tell his friend felt the same way. There was something about remaining in the former prison camp that made them still feel like prisoners. It was like the tentacles of Sagan were only loosened, and they were not completely free.

When Patton's men liberated the camp, on April 29, Thomas and the other prisoners had to remain in the same stinking camp with its bugs and vermin praying they would soon be on their way home. It was now May. As the camp disappeared behind them, he was beginning to feel like freedom was only behind the next bend in the road. He knew he probably would not feel completely free until he returned to Chicago.

With every jar of the ambulance, he felt as if he was leaving the stench of prison behind. They soon arrived at the chaplain's unit. The chaplain helped them down from the ambulance. And Thomas and Barney gingerly felt their way into an area reserved for officers and any wounded before the men were sent back from the frontlines.

"We'll have to get you out of those rags," the chaplain said. "We'll rig a shower for you, get you some fresh clothes and delouse you."

Thomas and Barney followed him meekly to the temporary barracks. After being cleaned up and given some food they were assigned to some Army cots and allowed to sleep.

"These cots are like heaven," Thomas said as he stretched out on one of the beds. The following day the unit's commanding officer visited them. The chaplain accompanied him.

"We do you little good if you remain here," he said. "I think the best bet is to get you to Brussels. They'll have a base hospital there or close by. With what you've been through, you're going to need medical assistance."

Thomas wondered how they would get to Brussels if the unit were stationed near Moosburg. It seemed as if the decision and means were available. The unit's officer explained that there were several men who'd received battlefield commissions and would have to go to Brussels to receive their new uniforms and be formally commissioned.

"They'll take you across Germany, through Bastogne and then on to Brussels. You think you're up to a trip like that?"

For the second time in two days Thomas and Barney answered in unison.

"Yes, sir!"

They relaxed as best they could that evening, but couldn't help notice the stares of some of the soldiers in the unit. There was a look of shock and anger in their eyes when they discovered the two former airmen had been POWs.

"We must really look bad," Thomas whispered to Barney as he observed the reaction.

Barney nodded.

They had not thought about their appearance because they were in a camp where all the other *Kriegies* had the same look. To be back with a unit where the men were physically capable of marching, fighting and carrying the war to the Germans was like entering a different world. It was a world that they'd been cut off from for too long.

For the first time, Thomas began to see himself as others now saw him—weak, thin and almost emaciated. He and Barney climbed into the back of the 4 by 6 truck for the journey to Brussels. They might be suffering the after effects of prison life, but no one was going to prevent them from taking this step toward home.

As Thomas and Barney traveled west toward Brussels they began to understand the full havoc of the fighting. Town after town was either bombed out or damaged from artillery and tank fire.

"I knew we were successful in our bombing raids," Thomas said as they rode through village after village in Germany. "But I didn't think that so many cities and villages were destroyed during the fighting."

"Nor I," Barney muttered.

"There's barely a wall standing in some of these towns," Thomas observed as he scanned the ruins of one town. A part of a wall here, a pile of bricks and concrete there, even the trees had been uprooted in one park and he saw some older women hoeing and planting potatoes and other vegetables.

"They'll have a crop from that park by winter," Barney said.

Thomas couldn't take his eyes off the city square. As they got out of the truck to stretch their legs, he noticed some middle-aged women trying to sweep away the mud and debris from the war. There were a few older men and some young boys. However, most cities were devoid of any men of military age.

"The men must be either prisoners or dead," Barney said.

The soldiers in the truck that accompanied Thomas paid scant attention to the women. They were more concerned about getting back to Brussels, obtaining their commissions and returning to the front.

"You guys have got to eat and drink plenty of water," one non-commissioned officer told them. "You're like walking skeletons. We want to fatten you up a bit before we get you to Brussels."

Thomas grunted acknowledgement and reached for some K-rations. He knew the soldier was right. Yet, he found it hard to eat the standard Army food. His stomach seemed to rebel against eating more food. He had drunk water for so long to calm the hunger pains as a prisoner, he couldn't easily tolerate the extra food he now received.

As the 4 by 6 truck continued on its way, Thomas saw a barbed wire encampment in the distance.

"What's that?" he asked the driver.

"A prisoner-of-war camp," the driver answered. He slowed to a stop near the gate. "But this camp is full of Jerries."

"No kidding," Barney said.

"I've been on the receiving end of the German camps. It's almost impossible to think of them being the prisoners now," Thomas said.

"Thought you'd feel that way," an NCO said. "That's why we stopped. It's about time you see someone else on the other side of the wire."

Thomas and Barney gingerly approached the guards at the gate. The driver of the truck disembarked and walked up to the sergeant at the entrance, all the while gesturing toward them. When the ex-*Kriegies* got closer, they overheard the driver.

"These guys have been prisoners at Sagan, went on a march during the dead of winter and ended up in Moosberg. They should see where the Jerries are now."

The sergeant looked in their direction and came closer. Thomas felt funny as the man took in their gaunt features and the clothes that hung from their frames.

"Come on in guys," the sergeant said. "You deserve to see what's become of the German supermen."

Barney and Thomas exchanged a look and walked reluctantly into the camp. There they saw the disheveled former soldiers of the Third Reich. The look in their eyes and faces was the look of men who'd been stripped of their mooring. No longer did they have the mesmerizing Adolph Hitler commanding them.

Thomas guessed there might still be SS men among them. Yet the majority probably had ceased to look upon war as a marvelous adventure where glory could be won.

As he stared at the Germans, he occasionally was met by a curious look from the prisoners.

Were they wondering who these strangers were? Maybe. Some may have even recognized that the men who'd been allowed into the camp were former prisoners. If they did wonder why these gaunt strangers were allowed into a prison camp, they gave no clue to their thoughts. Instead, the German prisoners wandered around the vast enclosure of the prison camp, much as Barney and Thomas had wandered about the prison in Sagan.

25

Transport to Brussels

Thomas had had enough. Instead of rejoicing in seeing the other half behind the wire fence, all he wanted to do was leave the prison atmosphere behind. It reminded him too much of what he had experienced as a prisoner. He couldn't just leave. He could tell that the sergeant had something else in mind. He and Barney were escorted into a large room piled high with cameras, helmets, German Lugers and binoculars. There were even watches on one table.

"Take what you want," the sergeant said.

"No, I don't want the memory of what we went through to be there whenever I look at something like this," Thomas said.

"Nor do I," Barney said.

Thomas could tell the guard was disappointed. However, he seemed to understand that for Barney and Thomas, anything that had belonged to a German soldier would only be a bitter reminder of life in prison.

After lunch, the men scrambled back on the truck and continued their journey west. They saw many American troops moving to the East and knew that the soldiers were still fighting in Austria and Czechoslovakia. Thomas gazed at the troops who were constantly on the move through the western part of Germany. If he didn't see men moving steadily westward, he saw German refugees trying to escape the tumult around them. As the day wore on and afternoon shadows grew longer, they pulled up to a small village to search out a place to stay.

Thomas was exhausted. He slowly lowered himself down from the back of the truck. His legs were stiff. His arms were sore from the constant jarring that they experienced on the pock marked road. The truck handled the debris on the road easily, climbing over piles of dirt; sliding down narrow lanes of the villages they traveled through and fitting itself between the leftover walls of damaged buildings. The village they stayed in was not as damaged as some Thomas had seen and they took shelter near the center of the town in a dilapidated inn.

While two of the men stayed near the truck, Thomas and Barney found a small room to stay the night. There were no beds, just an empty enclosure. Still, they were at least removed from the constant jarring of the truck. They, and three of the soldiers, spread blankets on the floor and promptly fell asleep.

The following morning they left the village and took a side trip to the northeast to see Bastogne. As the driver approached the city, Thomas was again struck by the total destruction that lay before them. Partial walls stood caked with dust and debris. Bricks had fallen on the roadway and at times the truck barely squeezed by tumbled down walls. At one point the driver stopped at a point where they could overlook the city and they disembarked to silently walk through the bombed out town. After an hour's break, the driver motioned toward the truck and they climbed back into it. A few more hours and they would be in Brussels.

What then? Thomas wondered.

As they approached the city of Brussels, Thomas was relieved to see a living city. There were civilians and soldiers streaming through the area. It was a different feeling to see men and women on the street together. He covertly watched the people, seeing little sign of the strain that must have been a part of their everyday life prior to the Allied invasion.

The buildings, for the most part, were intact. The center of the town had cafes where people gathered. Thomas longed to join them. When the truck neared the center of town, the driver informed them that this was as far as he could take them.

"I have to take these men to get properly commissioned," he said. "After that, we're all going back to the front."

Thomas and Barney left the protection of the truck and warily stepped into the teaming city. They looked around once to wave their thanks to the driver and the others, but they were far in the distance.

"What do we do now, Thomas?" Barney asked. "We have no money. We're just out here with the crowd."

Thomas thought he saw a military policeman in an area beside one of the cafes.

"I guess we'll have to report our whereabouts to someone, Barney. Let's see what that man recommends."

Thomas approached the police officer as Barney followed close behind. He soon realized the man was British, not American.

"Sergeant," Thomas addressed him. "We're former prisoners of war. Do you know where we should report."

The MP looked them over briefly, taking in their gaunt features and exhausted demeanor. "I will find out, gentlemen. If you will accompany me, I'll take you to my commanding officer."

Thomas and Barney fell in behind the man, following him to his headquarters. There, they explained that they had been driven across Germany from Moosberg to Brussels.

"Your own men just left you in the center of town?" a major asked.

"Yes sir. They were going to return to the front," Thomas said.

"No excuse for that. They should have taken you to their headquarters," the major said. He turned to a lieutenant and ordered him to take down their names and units. "We'll delouse you, give you a shower and some clean uniforms and money," the major continued. "Then you can relax while we find out where you go from here."

"Thank you, sir."

A surgeon took them aside after they were provided with clean uniforms. "It's about time you men had something to eat. After you eat I would suggest you go to bed early. We'll provide a place for you to sleep tonight."

Thomas and Barney readily agreed to spend the night at British headquarters. They were exhausted and the thought of a quiet place and sleep was overwhelming. As soon as they were guided to their temporary quarters for the night they took off their shoes and sprawled on the cots. In a few minutes they were sound asleep.

The next morning, after a breakfast like Thomas remembered tasting when they left the base in England, they again reported to the surgeon for further examination and instruction. He quickly checked them out and sat down across from them.

"You both know that you have been virtually starving as prisoners," he began. "I dare say you look to be skin and bones. I checked your weight and neither of you are over 130 pounds. You're weak and vulnerable. Having too much food can be a disaster at this stage in your lives. You have to be careful and gradually build up your strength."

"You'll be able to relax a little downtown," the surgeon continued. "But don't overeat. Above all, don't drink. From the look of you, you haven't eaten decently for a long time. If you try to eat too much or drink, you could kill yourselves. We've had a few former prisoners do exactly that."

Thomas and Barney found their way to a café in the downtown area. The two former *Kriegies* sat down and ordered some food. As they were observing the people in the street and the café, an announcement was broadcast on a nearby radio. It quickly spread through the town.

"The war is over. Germany's surrendered."

Thomas hugged Barney. Oh how he wanted to lift a stein of beer to the occasion and the café owner came over with drinks for them.

"It's on the house," he said happily. "I can't believe it's over. Come join our celebration."

"I wish we could," Thomas said as he stared at the brew the owner was tendering him. "But we can't. We just got out of a prison camp and were warned to not drink or overeat."

"But surely you can celebrate this great event?" the man persisted.

"You enjoy it for us," Barney said. "Believe me, we'd join you if we could. This is one event that I want to celebrate."

"George, they're right," a woman at a nearby table said. "It would be bad for them."

"Ah well," the man said. "'Tis a pity."

"Thank you, Ma'am," Thomas said. "I fear he doesn't quite believe us."

"Do what you need to do," the lady said. "There will be time enough for celebrating when you've regained your health."

Thomas watched as men and women drank and saluted the event. He and Barney sat, envying the joyous celebration, but not daring to become directly involved. Finally, they decided to return to the British base and wait out the event there.

"You followed orders," the surgeon said when he saw them. "I know you wanted to take part in the events of today, but you are better off here."

'I hope so," Thomas said. He could hear the laughter and cheers close by.

"Believe me, you are," the surgeon repeated. "Some former prisoners were in the downtown area, like yourselves. And they died. They couldn't resist drinking a toast to the end of the war."

Thomas and Barney exchanged glances. "I hope it wasn't anybody we knew," Thomas finally said.

"I hope so too," the surgeon said. "Meantime, get some sleep. You'll stay here a couple of days and then we'll put you on a train for Camp Lucky Strike, south of Le Havre. That is where they are gathering all former prisoners of war before sending them home."

A few days later, Thomas and Barney found themselves placed on a train bound for the camp. The trip by train was short. When they arrived, they found a tent city awaiting them. As Thomas walked into the area that now housed thousands of RAMPS (Recovered Allied Military Prisoners), he wondered when he would be allowed to go home.

26

Camp Lucky Strike

Who ever said the Army moved on its stomach was wrong, Thomas thought. The Army, Air Force, Navy and Marines must move in triplicate. Before he could even settle into a tent with other prisoners, he had to fill in paper work and more paper work. Almost immediately after the transfer to Lucky Strike, he was evaluated by medical personnel and then interrogated about his experiences after being captured.

"It's endless," Thomas complained to another prisoner. "They'll have us fill out one set of forms, then come back with another set. And, if I'm correct, I will be seeing these same doctors and nurses day after day."

"You're right there," the other prisoner said. "Then, when you get interrogated by intelligence, you'll have to answer every question they think of for some file back in the States. I bet no one even looks at those files."

Thomas pondered how to respond. Each person had been through something different. He'd been in Sagan and he'd already mentioned seeing the urns that held the ashes of the British who had tried to escape that camp before his arrival. Few had succeeded in making it back to the Allies. When he had arrived, the repercussions from that escape attempt were still felt.

"I think the Germans are going to have a lot to answer for in this war," Thomas said. "There's not only the war itself. There's the execution of helpless prisoners and look what they did to the Jews. Were you in Sagan? Did you see some of the flyers that were shot down, then forwarded on to the concentration camps? I did. I won't forget the stories they told. Nor, will I ever forget the march they put us through at the end of January."

"No, I wasn't in Sagan," the other prisoner responded. "But we had our share of problems with the Jerries. I don't think anyone here was immune. I hadn't heard about that march. What was it?"

"It was literally a death march," Thomas answered. "The Germans forced us to leave Sagan during the worst spell of winter in 50 years. I don't know how many died on the march. I don't suppose I'll ever know. But I've heard some say that it was worse than what happened in Bataan."

"Yeah, I heard of that one. Pretty bad."

"I have a brother, a prisoner of the Japanese," Thomas said. "Hopefully he survived and we'll both be home soon."

"My guess is that they'll forget what they want to forget," the other prisoner said.

"I doubt the British will forget the men who were executed by the SS," Thomas said.

"You may be right there," the prisoner said.

After the initial paper work was completed, Thomas and the other former prisoners spent their time relaxing, sleeping, visiting and looking for prisoners that they'd lost track of when the Germans moved them to Moosberg. For Thomas, Nuremberg and Moosburg were the worst experiences of his life.

He still couldn't believe how close the bombers came to the prisoner of war camps, yet managed to avoid hitting them. The designations that had marked the North, South, Central, East and West compounds of Sagan, merged into Camp numbers at Nuremberg. There had still been the barbed wire that seemed to mark every POW camp. Then, after the long journey to Moosburg had come the interminable waiting to be freed.

Thomas wondered how often he'd relive the memories of being a prisoner. He hoped one day he would be able to forget his experiences. However, in another sense, he never wanted to forget his life as a *Kriegie*. It made freedom that much more precious.

He already knew one aspect of that life that would always be with him, he couldn't stand being in a small room with no light. It was a reminder of his days in solitary confinement, when he was questioned before being transferred to Sagan. At Sagan, he hadn't been as aware of it as much as he was now. Nor, did it bother him in Nuremberg or Moosburg.

Perhaps it was because the Germans always used searchlights at night to scan the area for any prisoner who might dare to make an escape attempt. The lights often found their way into the barracks enclosures so that the interiors were not completely dark. The way they illuminated the buildings, it would be hard for the Germans to miss any movement away from the shelter of the barracks. The *Kriegies* had learned the hard way to not even stand in the doorway at night. A few of the men had been killed as they stood looking into the evening and the encampment.

At Camp Lucky Strike there was no longer the false darkness that had enveloped the camp. Instead, a true darkness often occurred with all its fears and memories of the cost of war lurking in the shadows of his memories. Thomas would gaze out at the stars some nights or take part in conversation with friends. Some of the men, in the camp, looked as if they could never forget what had happened to them. They'd bear the mark of war all their lives. Now they only waited to be shipped back to a hospital in the states.

Thomas wanted to concentrate on the now and the future. It meant leaving memories of the life in prison behind him. The now meant becoming accustomed to a life where he would eventually set the parameters of his own being and not have them set by guards, or the military. Camp Lucky Strike was a temporary interruption to his journey home to Marie. He would concentrate on the camp and face each day as it came. For him, he had learned the importance of living one day at a time.

During the days and nights there were all sorts of entertainment, movies, USO performances and the quiet security of knowing that they would soon be leaving for home. The medical personnel kept a constant eye on the prisoners, looking for signs of disease before it struck the weakened prisoners. In an attempt to have the former prisoners regain lost weight, they made eggnog and placed it in galvanized GI garbage cans throughout the base.

The former *Kriegies* were encouraged to drink all the eggnog they wanted. The only problem with it was it was made out of powdered milk, powdered eggs, a little cinnamon, but no liquor. It was one of the worst drinks Thomas had experienced during the war. However, like the other prisoners, he drank it, hoping that it would help him gain weight.

Each day some of the prisoners learned when they would be sent home and Thomas longed for his name to come up on the list. When it did, he'd wire Marie and tell her. The day came. He was finally told the exact date and time he was to leave.

At last, Thomas thought. Only a few days more and I'll board a ship home. A day or two before he was scheduled to depart, he went to shave himself. As he looked in the mirror at the gaunt face that stared back at him, he felt lightheaded. While he stared at himself in the mirror, he thought, I don't look right.

Thomas started to lift the razor to his chin, then, pulled it down. He felt unsteady. Something was wrong. He placed his hands on the sink to steady himself and again looked in the mirror.

It's my eyes, Thomas thought. There's something wrong with my eyes. His eyes looked different. The whites weren't white like they should have been—and suddenly he realized what was bothering him about his appearance. His eyes were yellow. He wiped off the shaving cream and slowly made his way to the medical center.

"I don't feel right....," Thomas started to tell one of the doctors. The doctor didn't wait for him to continue. Instead, he signaled to another doctor and a nurse. "Get this man to isolation. He's got yellow jaundice."

Later, the doctor explained, "The jaundice can be a sign of infectious hepatitis. We don't know if it's infectious or not. We'll know when the lab tests come back."

"But what about my going home?" Thomas asked.

"You're going nowhere. Not until you're treated. Hepatitis can spread."

Thomas weakly acquiesced. He couldn't do anything else but follow their orders. He found himself hustled to a field hospital nearby where he was isolated from other prisoners.

The doctors and nurses did not come into the tent where he was placed without thoroughly covering themselves in sterilized gowns. In the tent, Thomas found himself under 24 hour nursing care. After a week in isolation, he was finally permitted outside his solitary medical confinement. It would be an opportunity to intermingle with other patients and be a part of life outside a medical isolation tent. He decided the first thing he'd do would be to see a movie. One of the nurses wheeled him into the makeshift theater. He sat there feeling weak but at least he was somewhat a part of life in Camp Lucky Strike.

As the movie rolled on Thomas felt as if he was spinning out of control. He started to call out to a nurse.

"I....."

He felt himself pitching forward. Hands reached toward him, shoved him back into the wheel chair and took him back to the isolation tent.

As soon as he came around the following day, he found out he was being transferred to a French hospital in Rouen taken over by the U.S. Army. When he arrived at this hospital, Thomas joined five other patients who were former prisoners and were suffering from hepatitis as well. All of the men were placed on a very restricted diet to gradually regain their strength.

While there, Thomas felt well enough to walk around the hospital. He went outside and the scent of freshly baked bread wafted through the air. In his mind's eye, he could picture the scents of the bakery in Greek town in Chicago. He determined to follow the scent and soon discovered a bakery near the hospital that prepared food for the patients.

Walking in the door, he identified himself as an officer and demanded a large roll and loaf of bread.

"You can't have it," one of the bakers said. "You're a patient and probably on a special diet."

"My diet is of my choosing," Thomas said. He reached for a loaf of warm bread. Grabbed it and walked out the door. All the while, biting into and savoring the scent, taste and feel of the bread. He leaned against the wall outside the hospital. It was as if he had found a little corner of heaven when he discovered the bakery. However, he decided to keep the knowledge of the bakery to himself. If the other patients found out, there'd be too many of them making their way down to abscond with the rolls and pastries there.

He returned to his room feeling completely satisfied with the day's walk. He felt no ill affects from the treat. Instead, he felt as if he'd overcome one more hurdle in his journey back to good health. He could eat something that was not strictly hospital food and not be sick from the experience.

Thomas and the others continued waiting for word on when they'd be shipped back home. After a few weeks, he and the others were taken to the harbor at Le Havre and shown the hospital ship that would take them back to the states.

"That ship can't be any bigger than the ships I've seen on Lake Michigan," Thomas observed.

"I haven't seen Lake Michigan," another prisoner said. "But it does seem small."

"Small, but fast," a doctor said. "It's clearly marked as a hospital ship. There shouldn't be any problems now that the Germans have surrendered. You guys will be back in the States before you know it."

Thomas looked longingly at the ship. Here was his passage home. He wouldn't be arriving back in the States with the regular troops. He'd be with others who had suffered the ill effects of war. Still, it was only a day away and he couldn't wait for the night to pass so he could board the ship in the morning.

"Oh, incidentally," the officer continued, "you'll not be part of a convoy. Those babies move fast and there really isn't a need now. I can tell you that as officers you'll be sharing a stateroom with one other officer. Who that is will be made clear tomorrow."

Tomorrow. Another trip to this dock and he would be on his way home.

27

Journey Home

On board the hospital ship, Thomas shared a stateroom with an artillery officer. The room itself was not large. Thomas looked around the stateroom. Their quarters were neat and compact—two beds, a dresser, some closet space, a couple of chairs and a narrow shower room and a toilet. Plenty of room, he thought, especially when I think what the Germans gave us in Sagan and in the other prison camps.

A window at the end of the cabin allowed the men to look out upon the ocean as they steamed back to the States. Just beyond the cabin window were railings encircling the deck. When Thomas boarded the ship, he'd seen the large red cross on the ship's side and on the ship's smoke stack.

He realized he was fortunate to have the quarters he had. He knew other quarters were more cramped and those that were more severely wounded only had portholes looking out to sea. The sound of the engine was discernable in the room and as he looked back to shore, he could see a trail of black smoke coming from the ship's stack. The ship was still in the process of readying to depart to sea.

As Thomas scrutinized the man assigned to the cabin, he thought, I know this man from somewhere. I've seen him before. He soon learned his new roommate had attended Officer Candidate School at Fort Sill, Oklahoma, at the same time Thomas was there. It was then that Thomas had made the decision to resign so he could follow his dream of becoming an Air Corps cadet.

"You were fortunate you took the opportunity to become a cadet. Most of the people in our class were sent to the Asian theater and either killed or wounded," the artillery officer said. "I was wounded, returned to the U.S. and then sent over to Europe. The Germans captured me in their counter-attack last December. The conflict they now call—the Battle of the Bulge"

Thomas fingered his German Stalag Luft 3 dog tag. As he did, he remembered that there was a seam down the middle. If a person was killed in battle, part of the dog tag was broken off and sent back to confirm a death. The other part of the dog tag stayed with the deceased soldier. When he was freed, he'd removed the German Luft 3 tag and placed it in his pocket.

Some of the other prisoners had thrown their German IDs away as soon as they were freed. Thomas kept his. At the time, it seemed important. Now, he wondered, why he had kept an identification tag that reminded him of the torment of being a prisoner. The German guards required it to be worn at all times. He then placed his hand over the American dog tag around his neck. Both IDS marked a period of his life spanning almost five years. He switched his attention back to the conversation with his new roommate.

"I guess only one of my family ended up in the Pacific," Thomas said. "I spent almost a year as a guest of Hitler. I certainly wouldn't have wanted to be a prisoner of the Japanese. My youngest brother, Fred, was captured at Bataan. I haven't heard about him since his capture. I wonder how he's faring. The war is almost over in the Far East."

"You haven't received any word?"

"No."

The artillery officer changed the subject. Neither of them wanted to spend too much time discussing their experience as prisoners.

"Why don't we explore the ship after dinner," the artillery officer suggested. "The ship's small enough, I think there's only two decks below us, so it should be a quick trip to see the lower decks, just something to pass the time"

"I've heard the wounded enlisted men are on those decks," Thomas said. "Haven't seen anything of them though."

If we grab an early dinner, we can just relax for the rest of the evening, he thought. He wasn't in the mood to do much more. "Why don't we wait until tomorrow," Thomas suggested. "That will give us time to relax and we'll have something to do tomorrow."

"Fine with me," his new roommate responded.

They put some of their gear away and left the cabin in the early afternoon to join other officers and crewmembers topside. It felt restful just walking around, talking and getting to know the crew, other officers and the doctors and nurses. Thomas walked to the ship's railing and stared at the activity of the port. Although he couldn't see the tug, he knew that the ship was slowly following the lead of a smaller boat guiding it toward the open sea. He felt the waves slapping against the sides of the ship as it made its way out of the harbor. For almost an hour, he stood watching Europe fade into the distance.

"I may come back," he said as he continued staring at the coast of Europe. "But it won't be soon. I've seen too much to risk a return until Marie and I can find the time together."

Thomas remained motionless, looking, but also feeling, the waves that closed around the ship. He was surprised how peaceful he felt. Yet, he was still weak. He had only gained about 10 pounds since being freed from the Germans. His weight continued to fluctuate. If Marie were to see him now, he knew she'd be distressed. He'd left the States weighing about 185 pounds. Now, he weighed almost 130.

The weight wasn't coming back quickly. The doctors in Rouen had told him it would take time. He continued to eat and was never late for a meal. However he knew he must look like a specter in uniform. He was nowhere near his weight before his capture. Perhaps he had weighed less than 120 pounds when he and the other freed prisoners reached Camp Lucky Strike. He wasn't sure.

But, that was thinking too much about what was. He had to think about the future. And that future meant returning as soon as possible to a normal life. One thing he knew. He'd eat whatever was put in front of him. He turned and found the former artillery officer close beside him. As if by mutual consent, they left the rail and joined the other officers for dinner.

The evening passed pleasantly and Thomas and his roommate returned to their cabin. They talked briefly then settled into their beds for the night. Thomas couldn't sleep. Perhaps it was the excitement of being bound for home. He looked out the window at the waves and saw that daylight had long since disappeared from the horizon. In its place, was the blackness of the sea. The only hint of light on that vast expanse of water was the white foam that topped the ocean waves. Even in darkness, the foam from the waves was still visible. Finally, he drifted off to sleep.

After breakfast and some strong black coffee, Thomas and the artillery officer decided the time was ripe to investigate the lower decks. As they descended into the lower levels, Thomas saw another side of the war in Europe—its ugliness. The wounded on these decks lay there wrapped in gauze and dressings. Some had bandages around missing legs or hands. Others had their sleeves pinned to their chests. Faces looked up from their beds—their heads wrapped with gauze and compresses. He could see where eyes were missing and faces burned so badly he had to look away.

"I don't know what I expected down here," Thomas said, "but it wasn't this."

He felt guilty even walking around the wounded veterans. They were scarred for life. What type of an existence awaited them on their return home? Prostheses? Could they learn to adapt to no arms, no legs and the disfigurement that war had committed on them?

"Let's get out of here, Thomas," the artillery officer said. "They don't need to see us exploring their private hell."

Thomas started to turn around and retrace his steps. As a doctor came through, he asked, "Doc, how many wounded are like this?"

The doctor paused. "Too many. The rest of the decks below this are filled to capacity with amputees."

"And I thought prison camp was bad," Thomas said.

The two officers returned to the upper deck. Each of them had seen part of the war from different perspectives. Now they saw the gory spectacle of war's wake. And the wake was like nothing they had imagined.

"I don't want to see that again," his roommate said.

"Me neither," Thomas said as they slowly made their way back to their stateroom. When the two men closed the door behind them, each sat down on a chair lost in their own thoughts.

The days passed slowly and except for their incursion below deck, Thomas and his roommate almost felt as if they were on a pleasure jaunt.

About three days into the trip, a storm hit. Thomas had never seen a hurricane. However, the tossing of the boat, the churning waves around the hull and the constant riding up to the top of a wave, then sinking down on its other side convinced him that this storm had the power he associated with a hurricane.

The captain of the ship reassured them, "It's only a bad storm. We'll be out of it soon."

However the storm had the effect of making almost all the crew and passengers sick. Thomas and the artillery officer were the exceptions. They were not fazed, in the least, by the experience. Each day they made the journey to a small cabin that served as a mess hall, and ate what they could. No storm would keep them at bay during mealtime.

"We're probably the only ones enjoying the food," Thomas laughed after a particularly long dip between waves.

"Well, those that must have made it to the side have a distinctly green hue to their faces," the artillery officer commented.

There were not too many even making that effort. The waves were too treacherous and the captain advised all to stay inside their cabins during the storm.

After a day-and-a half, the storm passed and the other officers began emerging from their cabins. The deck was a bit slippery but at least they could take advantage of the fresh air. The hospital ship was close to the port of New York and

Thomas was looking forward to stepping ashore and seeing 'Broadway.' However, as they drew within sight of the city, the ship cut its engines to allow two troop ships to precede them into the harbor.

Thomas watched with envy as the larger ships steamed past. He heard bands playing in the distance. He saw fireboats spraying water in the air in an exuberant welcome to those returning from battle. He also saw the eager troops leaning over the rails, taking in the fireworks and festivities that awaited them. He imagined what it would feel like walking with his buddies in a ticker-tape parade. It was a pleasant thought and he waited for the captain to follow the ship in, but the hospital ship didn't follow the larger ship. Instead, it veered away from the troop ships and slowly made its way toward the New Jersey coast.

"We've been ordered to let the troop ship pass," the captain explained. "We're to pull into a dock away from the troop ship tonight. Then, you'll be taken directly by train to Fort Dix."

"Why won't they allow us to join those troop ships?" one officer asked.

The captain didn't answer. Instead, he retreated toward the ship's helm leaving the disappointed men behind him.

"But of course," the officer answered his own question. "The armed forces don't want the people to see the wounded, or the former prisoners that were half-starved fighting the Germans. It would ruin people's view of how noble war is."

Thomas looked toward the harbor of New York. So close. Yet, so far, he and the others could not join the Army troops returning home. Instead, they would be shuttled off under cover of darkness to a hospital. No one would see them disembark. They would disappear into the night, safely out of view.

"Oh, I'm sure they'll say that medically it's better for us to go directly to the hospital. But why can't they at least allow us to feel the same welcome those other soldiers are feeling?" Thomas vented his disgust.

He and the other officers returned to their cabins. There they sat until they docked. Then, they were loaded onto trains and taken to Fort Dix.

In the dead of night, the former prisoners and wounded veterans arrived at the hospital at Fort Dix, New Jersey. No brass bands greeted them. There were no family or friends to welcome them home, just the anonymity of the wounded going to a veteran's hospital. Thomas was among the walking wounded. It felt a little strange to set foot on American soil after winning a war and have stethoscopes, blood tests and doctors waiting for him instead of any of his brothers or Marie.

It was late and there was no opportunity to call her. All he'd been able to do since being freed was to send Marie a telegram that he was okay and couldn't wait to see her. It seemed strange to be cut off from loved ones. For all Marie knew, he was still in Europe awaiting passage home.

He should be happy he was on American soil, he told himself. Just because no brass band had met him or the other men who had been wounded was no reason to forget that he had survived the war and was home.

Like his fellow *Kriegies*, he would have to spend a few days at the New Jersey hospital. The stay would be brief. This much they were promised. When he was finally back in the Chicago area, he'd contact Marie.

Thomas settled into his hospital room, was duly checked over, and then assigned to a hospital plane to fly into Midway. Midway airport was almost an extension of Chicago itself.

Midway! That was his destination. Then he'd be taken to some place called Gardner General Hospital. When he arrived there, he'd be a step closer to Marie. Only a phone call away. Would it be better to call her? Or, would it actually be better to see her in person? He'd decide that later. Now, all he wanted to do was take off for home.

Thomas waited impatiently for the final leg of his journey home to begin. Even then, it would only be a stepping-stone to being discharged. The day came. On July 2, 1945, Thomas sat in a propeller driven hospital plane looking over Lake Michigan as the aircraft approached Chicago's main airport. Midway had a passenger section and an Army Air Force section. The Air Force section was located at the west end of the airport. It was there that the plane would land. He wondered how the other men felt. Were they as happy as he? Some were lying down on stretchers, nurses near by in case of an emergency. Others, like him, sat in seats, waiting anxiously for the journey to end.

As the plane descended, Thomas saw the city with its sprawled out houses and stores grow large against the horizon. The Lake looked blue and inviting. It had been years since he strolled along the city's beaches or caught a train into the city from the neighborhood where his grandmother lived. Marie would be living with her parents on Tripp Street. He imagined himself opening the door and wrapping his arms around her. He'd hold on to her and it would be the longest time before he'd let her go.

The plane banked and continued its descent. He felt the wheels touch down. The whir of the engines slowly decreased and soon the plane was moving at a good clip toward a hanger.

It was a bit bumpy, but not a bad landing at all, Thomas thought. When the plane stopped at the airport's west end, the pressurized door was opened and those on stretchers were carefully lowered to the ground. They were whisked away in ambulances toward the city. Thomas and those that were mobile rode in a bus toward the south side of the city, near Hyde Park.

"Gardner General Hospital is a former first class hotel," the driver said. "You guys won't even feel like you're in a regular hospital."

Thomas wasn't so sure of that. He'd been in a lot of hospitals since being a *Kriegie*. They all had a distinctive air about them. Gardner would be no different, he was sure. He entered the multi-storied hospital and glanced around to see nurses, doctors and orderlies rushing back and forth. Where there were doctors and nurses, there were needles and the pushing and probing of medical personnel.

He was checked into the hospital, assigned a room and taken by wheelchair to an elevator that slowly ascended to another floor. Finally he was deposited in his new quarters. A physician came in to assess his charts, which had also been forwarded with him to Chicago, then left. A short time later another doctor appeared and introduced himself.

"You've had a rough time of it and you're still extremely under weight," the doctor informed him.

"You should have seen me before, Doc. Now I weigh almost 145 pounds."

"We'll let you settle in, but tomorrow I want to go over your condition with you," the doctor said, almost as if he hadn't heard a word from his new patient.

"It's all there in the charts, doc," Thomas said.

"I know much of it is. But I think you should know how your experience as a POW has affected your health and what it means for the future. There has been a definite effect and it will take time for you to heal. Time enough to talk about that tomorrow. Meanwhile, try to rest. You'll be getting dinner soon. So, enjoy it."

"You mean enjoy hospital food?" Thomas asked.

"Well, sometimes it's possible. And, then, there again…," the doctor's voice trailed off. He shrugged as if to say, 'What do you expect?' Then smiled and left.

The next afternoon the doctor came back and sat down by Thomas's bed. "I said I'd talk to you about how your experiences have affected you. I think it's best to put the cards on the table. The lack of food and the march you were on has sapped more than your strength," the physician said.

He consulted a chart before continuing. "You're married aren't you?"

Thomas nodded. He didn't know where this was heading. What did Marie have to do with his experiences as a prisoner?

The doctor hesitated before continuing. "Your health has been affected to the extent that your imprisonment has had an effect on your ability to have children."

"What?" Thomas stared at him, shocked, disbelieving what he was hearing. He'd expected the doctor to just state the obvious—that he was underweight and he would have to be careful with what he ate until he regained his full strength. That was the scenario he expected, not this.

"Yes, it's true." The physician continued, "You won't be able to have children for some time. Your system has to return to its own stability, by that I mean, you have to get back to the point you were at before your imprisonment as a POW. That doesn't mean you will never have children. It just means that part of your life has to be put on hold for a while."

"I don't believe this," Thomas said more to himself than to the doctor. He looked up at the doctor, searching the physician's face to find out if what he was saying was actually true. And, as he stared at the physician, he began to slowly comprehend and accept the man's words.

"I said that part of your life will be on hold for a while, not forever," the doctor tried to blunt the harshness of his previous statement. "You and your wife will be able to have children eventually. However, it will not be the case for the foreseeable future."

"How long, doc?" Thomas asked. His voice was barely above a whisper.

"I'm not sure, but my opinion is it will be about ten years before you can expect that part of your life to continue."

"Ten years!" Thomas looked away. How could a year in a German prisoner of war camp do him so much harm? Or, was it the march? Maybe it was both.

"I'll leave you for now," the doctor said. "I'll check in with you tomorrow." He hesitated. Then, repeated, "Remember, this part of your life is only delayed. It's not forever."

"Ten years," Thomas whispered after the physician left him. Then the doctor's words sank in; "your life is only delayed." He hadn't let disappointment or obstacles defeat him before.

He would just make the best of his life now. He'd finish his education. He'd get a job. He'd set up a life for Marie and for that child of the future. And, when the time came, it would come. Marie would understand. They'd go through this setback together. He stood up and looked in the mirror. He was still thin, still gaunt from his year at Sagan. But, he could see he had gained weight. There would be hope for the future.

After several days in the hospital, Thomas was given leave to go home. He hoped he could remember the way. It had been almost two years since he'd seen Marie. He found his way to Tripp Street. There before him, was the small bungalow where Marie's parents lived. He hesitated, trying to find the right words to say.

He walked up the sidewalk and knocked on the door. There she stood before him, her slender figure framed by the doorway. Her red hair combed back. As he gazed at her, unable to speak for several minutes, he realized she didn't recognize him.

"Marie…"

Then, came recognition, "Oh, Thomas."

They stood there, holding on to each other, neither wanting to release the other from the other's grasp.

"Thomas, welcome home," Marie said as she guided him into the house.

28

Friendly Fire

Thomas still did not feel completely at home. He had to check into Gardner General Hospital each day, then return to Marie's home at night. It was a constant change from relaxing with his wife in the evening and then returning to the hospital during the day.

One day, while he was at home, Richard stopped by to see him. He, like his older brother, William, was still in the Armed Forces. However, William was stationed in Europe and Richard remained in Wisconsin. Thomas was anxious to receive word about his youngest brother, Fred, who had been captured by the Japanese and he hoped Richard had been able to learn something about his whereabouts.

As he hugged him in welcome, Thomas sensed the news about Frederick was not good. Richard didn't come right to the point about Fred. Instead, he kidded Thomas about his outranking him.

"You're going to have to salute me, big brother. I'm a captain. You're still a lieutenant," Richard said.

"I'll salute your rear end with a swift kick if you try to pull rank on me, Richard."

Thomas grinned as he appraised his brother's appearance. Wisconsin seems to have agreed with him, he thought. Richard has even put on a little weight. And, he's grown in confidence.

"Do you like Wisconsin, Richard? What are your plans?" Thomas asked.

"I'll finish my time in the service, Thomas. I'm not staying in Wisconsin. I'm going back to Bensenville."

"Bensenville?"

"Yes, it's my home. It's always been. You moved on to Chicago. Are you and Marie going to live here?"

"No, I don't think so," Thomas said as he straddled an arm on a leather chair while Richard relaxed on the couch.

Instead of talking over old times, there was a strained silence for a few minutes.

"It's Fred," Thomas spoke softly almost as if he didn't want to let the words out. "What have you found out?"

Richard looked down at his feet for several moments before responding.

"He's dead, Thomas," he finally said, his voice cracking with emotion.

Thomas sat stunned. He knew there was always a chance William or he would die in the war. Somehow, he never expected Fred to die.

"How?" Thomas asked, his voice barely above a whisper.

"Friendly fire." Richard stated.

"Friendly fire? How could he be killed by friendly fire? He was a prisoner."

"That's how," Richard explained. "He was a prisoner of the Japanese being shipped to Japan in an unmarked ship. The ship was torpedoed."

Thomas's face paled. He recalled the fear some of his buddies had of being on an unescorted hospital ship. Even though it was marked as a hospital ship, there was still the fear that a German U-boat might still be lurking. After his experience with the SS, their firing into the prison camp at Nuremberg to kill unarmed prisoners and their turning their guns on the old German guards who wanted to surrender. It was a real threat in the men's minds, especially if a member of the SS captained the submarine The captain might be aware of his country's surrender and determined to fight to the last man.

Somehow, it never had occurred to him that his brother would be on a ship that was torpedoed by his own countrymen.

"How did you learn about it?"

"One of the survivors was picked up. He and a few other American prisoners survived. He told me the majority of the prisoners were below deck and didn't stand a chance."

Thomas sat there, recalling how the four of them had stood together in Bensenville. Although they were in separate units at the orphanage, when a fight threatened one of them, they all came together to defend each other. He found it difficult to envision.

There would be no body brought home after the war. No coffin. No burial. Instead, Fred would remain beneath the seas near Japan.

Thomas put his head in his hands. As he sat there, he knew that he had been the lucky one. He had survived. He still carried the picture of Marie in his breast pocket.

It had stopped a bullet. But nothing could repel the hurt that he felt at Fred's death.

He sighed and looked over at Richard.

"What should we do?" Thomas asked.

"What do you mean?"

"Should we arrange for some marker or something at Bensenville?"

"Perhaps."

"You know that when William comes home we'll have to decide what to do."

"Let's face this in the future," Richard suggested.

"Does William know?" Thomas asked.

"Yes."

"Then, we'll have the rest of the family meet and decide what to do."

"What about you Tom?"

"Well, Marie and I are going to do some traveling. I'll get released from the hospital and we'll go west as soon as we buy a car."

Richard nodded, "A good idea," he said. "What then?"

Thomas stood up and began walking around the living room. "When I was a prisoner, I thought about continuing my education. I'm eligible for the GI bill. I always wanted to be an engineer. I'll go back to school."

"A plan, but you've been away from school for five years. Do you think you're up to it?"

"I've always been up to it, even when grandmother didn't think I was up to it."

"And how is grandmother?"

"She's well, but older. I've maybe seen her once or twice."

Again, they paused. Five years of war had pointed them in different directions. They should have much to talk about, catching up on their lives. However, maybe it would be easier once Thomas and Marie had settled on their own future and left the military behind them. It seemed as if Richard was of the same opinion, because he stood up and started to the door.

"Thomas, I'll see you again soon. I'll leave you now."

Thomas walked him toward the door. Marie would be home soon, as would her parents. He'd tell her about Fred and they'd make plans. Yet, he wished he could spend more time with Richard. Now was not the time.

"Let's get together again, Richard. I need to take some time to get the thought of Fred's death out of my system.

"I'll come down again. Meantime, keep in touch."

As he left, they could see Marie coming up the walk. Richard waved to her, then went on.

"Thomas," Marie said. "Why isn't Richard staying with us for the night?"

Thomas didn't answer at first. Instead, he escorted her back into the house, leading her to the kitchen. She waited while he put on a pot of coffee.

"He isn't staying because he wants to give me some time alone with you and later with your parents."

"Yes?" Marie's eyes widened as she waited for him to continue.

"Richard just told me that Fred was killed in the war in the Pacific."

"Oh Thomas, I'm so sorry."

"You didn't know him, Marie. But he was some fine kid."

"Kid?" Thomas laughed. "It's hard for me to think of him as being more than a kid. He was a Marine. He died while a prisoner of the Japanese. I never thought it would happen."

Thomas stood facing the sink. He took out two cups for the coffee and waited until it stopped perking. Poured the coffee, turned and placed a cup in front of Marie and one in front of himself.

"Marie, we put the money in the bank. I'm going to withdraw part of it and get a car. I have 30 days leave coming. I want us to go west, travel, see something of this country that I fought to defend."

"That sounds like a good idea," Marie said.

"I should be released in a week. I'm still considered a part of the Armed Forces until my discharge. After my release, I'd like to start by going down to visit the University of Illinois and arrange to start school in January. With the GI Bill and the money that I'm due, I think we can manage."

"That means we'll be leaving this house and moving, Thomas. You'll want to see your sisters and grandmother and Richard again."

Thomas nodded.

"Hopefully by the time we get back, William will be here and we can all get together. At least part of the family can start putting their lives in order," his voice broke and Marie placed her hand on his.

A U.S. Hospital ship like the "Acadia" transported Thomas to a harbor in New Jersey.

Thomas in 1945 after arriving home.

Thomas after graduation from the University of Illinois in 1947.

Marie, Tom Jr. and Tom Sr. in 1955 in Wheaton.

29

Ghosts of War

After his discharge from the hospital, Thomas received a month's leave. He bought a 1940 Plymouth. Then, he and Marie began traveling. He wanted to visit the families of his old crewmembers. It was as if seeing them was closing a chapter in his life. He felt a loyalty to the men he'd known in the service and by extension, their families. This trip would help lay the ghosts of war to rest.

The faces of the crew—Harold Niswonger, the pilot; Rod Steele, his friend and copilot; Thomas Fitzgerald, the bombardier; and Robert Morrison, the radioman—came to the forefront of his thoughts. Their faces did not change. Their visages remained the same as they were that fateful May when they were shot down.

Would he ever forget the other crewmembers—Ed Marsh, Albert Grick, Dale Johnson, Robert Robertson and John Caum? He hoped he never would. They had become bound together through the fire of war. They were now members of a far-flung family that included every man and woman who had served in the war. Because he knew them and flew with them, they were closer to him.

Thomas knew it would not be an easy trip. However, he felt bound to see the families of the men he had flown with over Germany. Maybe it would heal his own mind and bring some ease to the families of the men who died.

He'd already discovered that some components of his experiences in war would always remain with him. The shrapnel lodged in his back was a constant reminder of how close he had come to losing his life.

The interrogation where he found himself confined to a cell with hardly a trace of light during the day left its mark. Now, there had to be some light or a door that was open, a door that told him he was not a prisoner but a free man. There was the arm that the German doctors wanted to amputate. He'd managed to keep them from doing it. Yet, the scar from that wound again reminded him how lucky he had been. He kept the picture of Marie in his thin wallet. Her picture had literally come between him and a bullet. When he looked at it, he thought, how lucky he was to be alive.

Thomas and Marie first visited Robby Robinson in Beaver Falls, Wisconsin. Then, they went south and west to visit other crewmembers. Rod lived in Maine. They wouldn't see him this time. Caum never survived that day in May when the plane was shot down. Grick lived in Louisiana. The journey took the better part of October. Marie and he then returned to Chicago and Thomas reported to Fort Sheridan.

After a week with Marie's parents, he received orders to report to San Antonio to fill in paperwork for his discharge.

"Why I have to go there and can't be discharged here I'll never know, Marie," he said as he packed a few items for traveling.

"It won't be too bad, Thomas. At least I know you'll be through with the armed forces and we can begin a new life. And, I'll be with you."

"A new life, a new dream," Thomas said. He'd gained some more weight since coming back to Chicago, but not enough to keep his clothes from hanging loosely on his thin frame.

When they reached San Antonio, Thomas reported to the aviation cadet center that had been turned into a discharge center for returning veterans. It was a mass of humanity. Veterans, wounded and carrying the remnants of war within their own bodies, lined up to begin the process of changing from a life of war to the life of a civilian. As he gazed at the crowd, Thomas wondered if he and Marie would find a place to stay while he attended to the process of questions and paperwork.

They were fortunate that a friend who had also been a prisoner in Sagan allowed them to stay in his hotel room while he moved temporarily to bachelor's quarters. After Thomas filled in the necessary forms for his discharge, he decided to sign up with the Air Force reserves after they offered him an early promotion to captain.

"They'll give me a commission as a captain and the pay for that rank and being in the reserves could help us later," Thomas explained to Marie.

"I just wish you were done with it," she said. "The armed forces took almost five years out of your life."

"I know. But it will help us with additional pay while we map out our future. We'll not only receive money from the GI Bill, but a little extra because of being in the reserves. Remember, I plan on returning to school to finish my education."

After the discharge process was completed, Thomas and Marie returned to Chicago and spent Christmas in familiar territory. He was awarded another leave, this time for 60 days and they again spent the time traveling. Thomas attempted to find the sister of his pilot, Harold Niswonger, but finally gave up and Marie and he continued their journey west. They spent many weeks exploring the country from the Grand Canyon to the Rocky Mountains and on to the Pacific. They did not attempt to go far to the north because of winter cold and snow.

What they saw was a countryside that they knew would eventually change as life returned to a peaceful economy. Thomas envisioned new highways, bridges and roads, buildings dotting the landscape as towns grew and the population multiplied. What a time to be an engineer, Thomas thought.

On their way back to Illinois, Thomas and Marie stopped at the University of Illinois at Champaign-Urbana. Thomas registered at the university for the March semester. However, instead of being a civil engineer, he found that his wounds limited his original idea of constructing dams and bridges. He couldn't use surveying instruments because of his arm. Therefore, he signed up to pursue studies as a structural engineer.

The month in Chicago passed quickly. Marie quit her job at Sears and they moved down to the University of Illinois. They thought they had a house rented for the spring but when they arrived, they found the house was sold and the new owners would not allow renters. After a brief interval at a hotel, Thomas again came across an old friend from his first two years at the University, Dan Park from Metropolis, Illinois.

"I have a veteran's prefab," Dan informed Thomas. "You and Marie are welcome to stay with me while my wife has a baby. She'll be home in Metropolis for the next few months. You should sign up for veteran's housing. More of it will soon be available through the university."

Within a month's time, Marie and Thomas secured a one bedroom prefab house in Illini Village, east of the university cemetery. In this enclave for veterans and their families they found a home that allowed them time to not only have their own house but to consider where they wanted to live in the future. Champaign-Urbana had the atmosphere of a university town. However, it also gave them a taste of life outside the city and they agreed that when it came time to return to the area of Chicago, they would live outside the city.

Time seemed to rush forward. Marie began teaching English to returning veterans at the University and Thomas rushed to finish his studies. A woman professor tutored him in his second course in calculus. Five years before he had finished his first course. Now he found it difficult to recall the concepts he'd learned then. For Thomas, this was his hardest course. A fear of not being able to complete his studies for his chosen vocation soon gave way after several weeks to a realization that he could and would be able to obtain a degree.

Thomas completed his first semester of his junior year at the university. A year-and-a-half later, he finished his studies and had his choice of potential employers. He chose a position with Public Service Company of Illinois. The position allowed him to live and work in the suburbs. Mat Markle promised him $250 a month to begin.

When he reported to work at Oak Park, Markle came up to him and seemed embarrassed.

"Thomas, I made a mistake. The company won't pay you $250 a month. They'll only pay you $240. If you agree to stay on, I'll make it up to you."

Thomas didn't hesitate. To lose the $10 was a blow. However, he felt he could trust his new supervisor. So, he agreed. Within three months, his salary rose to $260 a month. Shortly after September 1947, he and Marie found their dream house in Wheaton. They purchased the home in the suburbs, with the help of a mortgage, for $12,000.

"This loan is based on your future potential," the bank officer told him. Marie obtained a job with the Chicago School Board. Thomas's earnings, though small, allowed him enough money to pay the mortgage, taxes and insurance of $76 a month. He was on his way.

The next two years went by swiftly. In 1949, the company began converting from manufactured gas to natural gas and houses within the suburbs had to convert to the new system. Thomas transferred to the design and engineering department and from there to the operating department. He moved up the ladder. Soon, he was in charge of converting homes within the suburbs to natural gas.

Time flowed by. In 1954, another milestone occurred in Thomas's life. It had been almost 10 years since the end of World War II and Thomas and Marie fulfilled another chapter of their lives. Marie gave birth to a baby boy, who Thomas promptly named Tom.

Thomas, Tom Junior and Marie began to meld themselves into the growing suburbs of Chicago. Marie quit working for the Chicago School System and Thomas resigned from the Air Force Reserves in 1967. He enrolled at the University of Chicago during the 1960s and obtained a master's degree in business administration from the University in 1969. The time he spent between his job, the Air Force Reserves and obtaining his degree eventually forced him to make a choice between the Reserves and obtaining that degree. He retired from the Reserves after 25 years of service with the rank of major.

Thomas also wanted to spend more time with his son. He remembered how much he had missed his parents when he was at Bensenville and he wanted his son to have a father who took an active interest in his growing up. He became involved in Boy Scouts and watched with pride as his son obtained the rank of Eagle Scout. As young Tom attended Scouts from grade school to high school, Thomas became more active in the Scouts' program and became a scoutmaster.

In the meantime, Tom Jr. graduated from Wheaton High School in 1972 and received an appointment to the Air Force Academy. As they were about to leave, Thomas sensed his son was reluctant to attend the Academy.

"You seem troubled at the thought of going to the Academy," Thomas said.

"Well, I know you always wanted me to go," young Tom said.

Thomas sat down in the living room opposite his son. He motioned Tom to a seat.

"Tom, this isn't about my dream. It's about your dream. If you do not want to attend the Academy let me know. I followed my own dream when I was young. I want you to follow yours. Now answer me. Do you want to go to the Academy?"

"No, Dad."

"Then, it's settled. You won't."

"You mean it?" Tom asked. "I don't have to go?"

"T. L. means it," Marie said as she unobtrusively came to his side. "We have always wanted you to do what you want."

"What do you want to do, Tom?" Thomas asked.

"I think I'd like to go to the University of Illinois."

Thomas and Marie exchanged a glance. "Like father, like son," Marie said.

His years with Public Service Company of Illinois brought advancement in his career. He worked his way up to become manager of construction, the very top of the middle management group. Thomas could not go any further in his career. He was caught in the politically correct atmosphere of the times. More women executives were needed in the executive suite. Although he felt prepared to go higher, he knew that he couldn't. He and Marie would concentrate on other aspects of their lives.

While he and Marie were visiting friends in Cincinnati in 1980, Thomas learned there was a reunion of prisoners of war from Stalag Luft III. He mentioned he was a former POW and would like to join the organization.

"If you're interested in this organization, you should also inquire about the 8th Air Force Historical Society," one of the members, Bob Weinberg, said. "It's been in existence since 1974. They're looking for former members of the 8th Air

Force. I know the Society is also planning a return trip to England later this year."

"Go back to England?" Thomas asked. He had wondered about returning and yet had never really spoken about it to Marie. He had fond memories of England. Yet, if he returned to England, he knew he would have to go beyond his old base and return to Sagan. There he would have to face the memories of his imprisonment and locate the graves of the men he'd known during World War II.

"To return to Europe after almost four decades," he told Marie, "it is like reopening a chapter of my life that I thought I'd left behind."

30

A Successful Life

Thomas and Marie made the trip to England in the fall of 1980. It was the beginning of a period in his life where he found new interests and challenges. He now looked both forward and backward—forward to becoming more involved with the veterans who had flown in Europe during World War II and had become prisoners in Sagan. When he looked backward toward that period of his life, his memories of the war became more vivid.

In 1981, he attended the 8th Air Force Historical Society meeting in Minneapolis. Attending another meeting in 1982 in Cincinnati, he and about 50 members of the Society determined to form the 96th Bomb Group. The group was formed to remember the men who had served with this branch of the 8th Air Force out of Snetterton-Heath from 1943 to 1945. Thomas was elected secretary/treasurer of the new group.

Then, came 1982. Thomas decided to retire from the gas company. He and Marie would enjoy the rest of their lives. They'd travel. He would remain active with the 96th Bomb Group. He envisioned creating a newsletter so the Group's members could keep in touch. He would also take a trip to Europe to see if he could find the graves of his friends who had never come back from the war.

In May 1985, he and Marie attended a tulip festival in Holland. It was Thomas's first trip back to the European continent. He wanted to find the graves of Niswonger and Knobby Walsh. They had been dead for over 40 years, but he had never forgotten them and never would.

They traveled beyond Holland tracing the cemeteries until they reached Liege. As Thomas and Marie approached the cemetery a grounds keeper stopped them. "What are you doing here? It's almost time to close."

"I've come to see a friend," Thomas said. He looked beyond the gate to the many crosses lined up like a battalion of death within the cemetery.

"So you fought here too?" the man nodded in understanding. "Who are you looking for?"

"His name was Walsh. We called him Knobby." Thomas tried to remember Walsh's real name. "His first name was John."

"Come with me and I'll check our list," the caretaker said. "Ah, here he is. Are you just going to visit the grave? You have no flowers?"

"I didn't think about that."

"I have a friend down the road. I'll call him. You can pick up some flowers and come back. I'll wait for you."

Thomas thanked him. Then, Marie and he sped back in the direction of town to find the flower shop. They arrived at the shop near closing time. As they entered, they discovered the proprietor, a man in his fifties, could only speak French. However, they managed to communicate that they wanted to buy some flowers.

The telephone rang and Thomas and Marie began to look around the shop. When the owner returned to assist them, he said he would help them pick out the flowers but would take no money for them.

"You and the people in the cemetery once fought for our freedoms. Therefore, I cannot accept payment," he said.

Though he spoke in French, Thomas was able to understand him. They picked out some brightly colored daffodils and the owner wrapped them in cellophane. Thomas and Marie thanked him and returned to the cemetery. The caretaker met them, then escorted them to the grave.

"I'll let you be alone," the man said. "So many graves. But we will always remember what you Americans did."

The caretaker turned and left. As Thomas and Marie stood near the grave, Marie looked toward the marker on the grave's right.

"Thomas?"

"Yes, Marie."

"This is strange. The grave next to Knobby's has the name of Walsh, William Walsh, on its marker."

Thomas had just knelt by Knobby's grave to place the flowers by the marker. Now he got to his feet and looked at the other grave.

"I wonder?" Thomas said. "I think Knobby had a brother. Here are two men with the same last name, who died at different times during the war. How can that be? Do you think this grave could really hold Knobby's brother?"

"I don't know. It is strange. Two men with the same last name. Take a picture of the two graves and ask Knobby's sister. She's still living isn't she?" Marie said

"Yes. But I haven't contacted her in a while." Thomas raised the camera to his eye and took a picture of Knobby's grave, then the other. Then, he took them both together. After a moment, Thomas leaned down, divided the flowers into two parts one for Knobby's grave and the other portion for the person named Walsh buried beside him.

They slowly retreated from the gravesite and as Thomas glanced back in the direction of the graves he could see row upon row of crosses. He hesitated by the gate. He knew he would not return.

Seeing the cemetery had closed a portion of his life. He could now look to the living and leave the dead to their solitude. Within a week, Thomas and Marie returned to the Chicago area. There, they called on Knobby's sister. Thomas wanted to give her a picture of the neatly kept grave. He'd also take the opportunity of asking her about the grave next to Knobby's.

Knobby's sister took the photograph of the grave and thanked him. She didn't look at the picture at first.

"I found something unusual when I visited that cemetery," Thomas began. He wasn't quite sure how to mention about the other grave.

"Yes?" she asked.

"Well, when Marie and I were there we noticed another grave next to his with the same last name, Walsh. Didn't Knobby have a brother? Could this be his grave?" Thomas handed her a second photograph. This one contained a picture of Knobby's grave and the one next to it.

She stared at the picture, then began to tremble and sob. "We never knew where he was buried, Thomas," she finally said. "He was in the Army. He died soon after Knobby. I would never have dreamed that they would be together in death."

She hugged Thomas and Marie and then continued to stare at the picture of her other brother's grave.

"I think we need to leave, Marie," Thomas whispered.

Marie nodded and they slipped out of the house. They returned to Wheaton and never saw Knobby's sister again.

Years passed.

Thomas had always felt he owed something to the German Evangelical Church that raised him in Bensenville. He determined to find a church of the same denomination in the Wheaton/Glen Ellyn area. He first joined the First Congregational Church in Glen Ellyn. Then when a new church, St. Matthew's United Church of Christ formed in Wheaton he became a member there.

The German Evangelical Church of his youth had merged with the German Reformed Church to become the Evangelical and Reformed Church. It later merged with the Congregational Church and became the United Church of

Christ. When he had first married Marie, he had told her and the priest marrying them that he would never leave that church. It had raised him and he would keep that promise to himself and Marie.

Thomas continued to remain active in the veterans' organizations. He was elected secretary/treasurer of the 96th Bomb Group. He became president of the 8th Army Historical Society, serving two years. He also helped found the Retired Officers Association that was active in the Wheaton area. The Retired Officers Association grew to over 300 members. The 8th Army Historical Society had over 20,000 members. Over time their numbers decreased. Those that had served in World War II were dying and a movement to honor their sacrifice was astir in controversy.

As the year 2002 emerged, a monument to the men of the 96th Bomb Group became a reality at their old base in England. Thomas and Marie went back to Snetterton-Heath for its dedication. They then returned to Wheaton. Age has crept up on the former navigator and his wife. However, they have not lost the hope and feelings that brought them together over 60 years ago.

Both he and Marie often frequent a restaurant in Wheaton—Alfie's—that was and still is a meeting place for the old timers of Wheaton who had spent a generation within the city. Yet, as that generation passes, others have found the restaurant and claimed it as their own.

One thing intrigued Thomas about the restaurant; it was named for the words from the song in the movie Alfie, "What's it all about, Alfie?" In a sense, his life had answered that question; what's it all about? He'd found that medals from the war meant nothing. What he was proudest of was gaining an education, graduating from the University of Illinois as an engineer, receiving his MBA from the University of Chicago, was an achievement his grandmother would never have dreamed he could attain.

His grandmother was gone. His brother, Richard had become mayor of Bensenville, but he too was gone. William was still alive, as was one of his sisters. They had all been through the crucible of war, each in a different way. Fred had died during the onslaught of war. Thomas and others now called their generation, "the greatest generation."

However, what Thomas most remembered about his life was the constant struggle to make something out of his life. As he looked back at his life as an orphan, then as a World War II navigator and as an engineer, he knew that he had achieved much. Perhaps he could have gone further in his life. Yet, he would never question what life had dealt him.

He had become an Air Force Cadet. He returned alive from the war when so many of his friends had died. Retaining the friendships over the years of the men he served with in the 8th Air Force counted as achievements and milestones in his life. He knew the importance of education and keeping on learning.

His son, Tom Jr., had that dedication to learning too. Young Tom had gone beyond his sojourn at the University of Illinois and like his father had obtained an MBA. However, his business degree was from the University of Michigan.

Thomas never gave up on his dreams. That is the lesson and the life of Thomas L. Thomas.

Epilog

Organizational activities after World War II

1946–1967	Member USAF Reserves (Retired as Major)
1966–1971	Scout Master—Troop 23—Wheaton, Illinois
1963–1969	Attended University of Chicago. Awarded MBA in 1969
1982–Present	Secretary/Treasurer—96 Bomb Group Assn.
1987–1988	President—The Retired Officers Assn. (West Suburban Chicago Chapter)
1990 and 1991	President—Eighth Air Force Historical Society
1995–Present	President—Eighth Air Force Memorial Museum Foundation

Bibliography

Primary Sources:

Oral History from Thomas L. Thomas.

The Longest Mission. The Association of Former Prisoners of Stalag Luft III, 1995.

Wright, Arnold A. *Behind the Wire: Stalag Luft III, West Compound,* 199?.

Secondary Sources:

Alf, Hertert A. *Petals of Fire.* Roseburg, Oregon: Millenium Memorial Trust, Inc., 1999.

Ambrose, Stephen E. *The Wild Blue: The Men and Boys Who Flew the B-24S Over Germany.* New York: Simon and Schuster, 2001.

Birdsall, Steve. *The B-17 Flying Fortress. Famous Aircraft Series.* New York: Arco Publishing Co., 1965.

Brokow, Tom. The *Greatest Generation.* New York: Random House, 1998.

Kennedy, David M. *Freedom from Fear: The American People in Depression and War, 1929-1945.* The Oxford History of the United States, Vol. IX. C. Vann Woodward, General Editor. New York: Oxford University Press, 1999.

Klaas, Joe. *Maybe I'm Dead.* Lincoln, Nebraska: iUniverse.com, Inc. 2000.

McKee, Daniel C. *A Kriegie Recall 50 Years Later Stalag Luft Diary.* N. Richland Hills, Texas: Smithfield Press.

Sirotski, Len. *The Bensenville Home: A Caring Community for Children and Old People.* Schaumburg, Illinois: Communities of Learning, 1995.

Tobin, James. Ernie *Pyle's War: America's Eyewitness to World War II.* Lawrence, Kansas: University Press of Kansas, 1997.

Watkins, T. H. *The Hungry Years: A Narrative History of the Great Depression.* New York: Henry Holt and Company, L.L.C. 1999.

0-595-33134-3